Jump Start Life Now

Skills and Principles *that Help Manage Living While in Crisis*

Learn Basic Tools for Successful Living During Recovery

MC Chapel Fellowship Edition

RECOVERY THROUGH CHRIST MINISTRY & PASTOR CHARLES PRETLOW

The LORD is near to the brokenhearted and saves the crushed in spirit. Psalm 34:18

Jump Start Life Now
Skills and Principles that Help Manage Living While in Crisis
Copyright © 2021 Charles Pretlow
MC Chapel Fellowship Edition

All rights reserved. Printed in the United States of America. No part of this publication may be reproduced, stored in a retrieval system, or transmitted, in any form or by any means electronic, mechanical, photocopying, recording, or otherwise, without the prior written permission of the author.

All scripture references and quotes are from the ESV is the English Standard Version ® (ESV®), copyright © 2001 by Crossway, a publishing ministry of Good Publishers. Used by permission. All rights reserved.

Other versions referenced and indicated as RSV Revised Standard Version of the Holy Bible unless otherwise noted. Old Testament Section Copyright © 1952 New Testament Section Copyright © 1946, 1971 by Thomas Nelson Inc.

Dedication, Acknowledgment, and Disclaimer

MCGM Recovery Through Christ Ministry and the author are grateful for the years of ministry the Lord has granted in helping wounded believers' recovery from a traumatized spirit, damaged emotions, and mental anguish.

For the hundreds of struggling Christians who came courageously to counseling sessions and recovery meetings through the years—who by faith sought the Great Physician's healing grace.

"'Those who are well have no need of a physician, but those who are sick. I came not to call the righteous, but sinners." Mark 2:17

The Lord saves the crushed in spirit. Psalm 34:18

We share these Biblical principles in the hope that with understanding you can now work with the Lord who is always near the crushed in spirit and the broken hearted. He has never left you, the problem is most hold him afar, not knowing how to let Christ in to heal and restore.

Indeed, He is the Lord of the wounded and lonely inside, if we let him in. If we learn to work with him to reveal and heal, to work with Him to show us what we can't or don't want to see within ourselves.

Disclaimer: This book, the author, MC Global Ministries, and Wilderness Voice Publishing are NOT a licensed mental health organization or individual mental health practitioner. Please read our full disclaimer on page 78.

ISBN 978-1-943412-12-9

Published by -
Wilderness Voice Publishing
Canon City, Colorado USA
www.wvpbooks.com

"A voice crying in the wilderness - proclaiming the good news of the coming Kingdom!"

Contents

Introduction	4
Recovery Bible Passages	7
When You Feel Overwhelmed	8
MCGM Recovery Through Christ Guidelines	9
Community Resource List	10
Personal Support Network	12

Jump Start Class Topics & Devotionals

1 Restoring Hope	13
Reigniting Your WANT TO?... 14	
2 Receiving Help from Others	15
Ask, Seek, Knock… 16	
3 Managing "Our" Anger	17
Patient Endurance… 18	
4 Relationship Boundaries	19
Distancing Game Player .. Evil Doers…20	
5 Recovery from a Wounded Spirit	21
Overcoming the Effects of Trauma…22	
6 Conflict Management	23
God sees Everything… 24	
7 Rational-Critical Thinking	25
Foolish Ideas and Low Self-Esteem… 26	
8 Pain Suppression/Addictions	27
Emotional and Spiritual Numbing… 28	
9 Effective Communication	29
Thoughts reveal issues of the heart… 30	
10 Rebuilding a Proper Self-Image	31
No more self-condemnation… 32	
11 God's grace and mercy	33
Turning over a new leaf?... 34	
12 Proper Perspective of Life	35
A Wounded or Broken Conscious?... 36	
13 Stress Management	37
Overcoming shame based living… 38	
14 Overcoming Learning Disabilities	39
Truth in the inward being… 40	
15 Identifying the Trouble-Maker	41
Avoid such people… 42	
16 Beware of Ooey-Gooey Evil	43
The evil-evil hides in a cloak of decency… 44	
17 Breaking the Family of Origin Spell	45
Temporary isolation therapy… 46	
18 Disturbing Thought Catching	47
Other's gunk cues our up our gunk… 48	
19 Overcoming Escapism	49
Pretending, Imagination, or Inspiration… 50	
20 Activating the Desire to Mature	51
Wake up and grow up… 52	
21 Forgiveness and Accountability	53
The Disease of Bitter Jealousy … 54	
22 Holding Ground While Advancing	55
Up and down at first, then steady progress… 56	

Personal Goals

Living Within Your means	57
Overcoming our Toxic Culture	60
Towards Making a Home	61
Cover Letter and Resume	62
Job Interviews & Presentation	64
Work Skills Development	65
Jump Start Job Search	66
Restoring Dreams…	68
Furthering Your Education	69
Parenting & Significant Relationships	71
Extended Family Relationships	73
Your Circle of Friends	74
Continued Recovery and Support	75
Fellowship and Spiritual Growth	76
About this Ministry and the Author	77
Ministerial Disclaimer	78

Jump Start Life Now
Introduction

MCGM Recovery Through Christ in conjunction with MC Chapel Fellowship provides this special edition of Jump Start Life Now workbook. Jump Start Life Now information and course curriculum were developed through years of experience in helping those in crisis restart life. The author and trained facilitators have gone through their own difficult challenges in recovery, learning to apply these principles.

Jump Start Life Now principles and skill lessons were derived from solid Biblical principles and Christ's teachings from the Gospels and the New Testament authors. You may not hold Christ as your personal savior, however, you will find that these principles and teachings are practical and when properly applied will help in overcoming difficult circumstances in life. Of course, these principles work more effectively when Christ's power is called upon to lead, guide, heal, and restore.

Refer to the Crisis Recovery Principles quick reference guide on the back cover. As you become familiar with these principles, and as you apply them, you can expect your inner attitudes to shift. Those inner glooming issues and expectations will begin to give way to hopefulness, with an increasing desire to become changed on the inside. Changing on the inside is the only way to break the destructive cycles that subtly lead people into crisis.

You can expect to learn how to replace inner lies, half-truths, and inner bitterness with truth—truth that is real, life changing, and freeing.

Jesus said, *"You will know the truth, and the truth will set you free"* **John 8:32**

Expectations and Opportunities

MCGM Recovery Through Christ ministry provides resources and a hardworking team to help you gain stability as you work towards putting your life back together. You will receive encouragement, help, and counsel—to help restore hope, your want-to, and the energy to overcome your situation.

We are a nonprofit ministry with limitations; however, we try not to let our limited resources deter you from doing your part in making progress. You will learn to work as a team with the others in your support group and group facilitators. Decide to take advantage of the help and opportunities available with our MC Chapel Fellowship staff, our services, and support network partners.

Jump Start Life—Life Skills Topics

Jump Start Life classes and Recovery Through Christ support group meeting are held on Monday evenings starting promptly at 7:00 lasting to 8:30. This workbook and lift skills topics are covered in the first 45 minutes, with the remaining half of meeting time dedicated to Recovery Through Christ support group work. During the Jump Start portion you are encouraged to take notes in the note section and journalize thoughts and questions after class. Don't hold back from asking questions or commenting during the Q & A portion of the class. Practice courtesy while others are speaking, and please raise your hand to participate. The topics are designed to help you grasp your situation and understand what went wrong and develop a course of action leading to recovery and learn how to avoid relapse.

Class Format

Each session will have a different topic shared by the facilitator that will include group interaction. Generally, in the beginning of each class, each person attending will have an opportunity to discuss their recovery progress. The following questions are guides in helping each person verbalize their progress. Please note the following reasoning for participating in this form sharing interaction:

- **One thing that you are grateful for today.**
  - **Reason:** It is easy to become bitter while trying to overcome a very difficult life situation. Taking time to consider at least one favorable or one helpful thing that occurred in your life during the day or during the week helps you to stay focused on your successes to maintain a hopeful attitude.

- **One accomplishment this week that helped in your recovery.**
  - **Reason:** Taking a mental survey of the day's accomplishments, whether the accomplishment was submitting a job application, a finished resume, or gaining insight on overcoming an addiction—by reviewing your day's accomplishments you instill a proper sense of progress and build confidence. As we gain confidence, the nagging negative and self-condemning thoughts begin to lose their ability to fuel hopelessness and depression.

- **One insight on <u>why</u> things went wrong and how to change the <u>why</u>.**
  - **Reason:** Few people fall into crisis without living in a pattern of repetitive chaos, conflict, and addictions that finally lead to a self-made disaster. Gaining insights to why cycles of dysfunction are repeated and how to break the cycles will put us on the road to living life successfully. These introspective questions help break denial. Denial takes the form of minimizing, rationalizing, blaming, and justifying our self-numbing behaviors, addictions and destructive behaviors. The negative things we practice in relieving our inner unresolved pain.

- **One thing you did to help someone else.**
  - **Reason:** Helping someone else who is struggling aids us in restoring our sense of purpose and community living. When we understand that we are not the only one struggling and learn to give a helping hand helps us get off our inner pain and self-pity treadmill. Making it a habit of helping others draws us away from self-centeredness and helps offset self-pity. A self-centered, self-pity pattern of living destroys our accountability to become mature adults in society.

Bible Passages to Help in Recovery

"The LORD is near to the brokenhearted and saves the crushed in spirit." Psalm 34:18

He heals the brokenhearted and binds up their wounds" (Psalm 147:3).

"Commit your way to the LORD; trust in him, and he will act." Psalm 37:5

"Submit yourselves therefore to God. Resist the devil, and he will flee from you. Draw near to God, and he will draw near to you." James 4:7-8

"For thus says the One who is high and lifted up, who inhabits eternity, whose name is Holy: "I dwell in the high and holy place, and also with him who is of a contrite and lowly spirit, to revive the spirit of the lowly, and to revive the heart of the contrite." Isaiah 57:15

"That according to the riches of his glory he may grant you to <u>be strengthened with power through his Spirit in your inner being</u>… Now to him who is able to do far more abundantly than all that we ask or think, according to the power at work within us, to him be glory in the church and in Christ Jesus throughout all generations, forever and ever. Amen" (Ephesians 3:16-21).

Christ spoke the following:

"The scribes said to his disciples, 'Why does he eat with tax collectors and sinners?' And when Jesus heard it, he said to them, 'Those who are well have no need of a physician, but those who are sick. I came not to call the righteous, but sinners.'" Mark 2:16-17

"Come to me, all who labor and are heavy laden, and I will give you rest. Take my yoke upon you, and learn from me, for I am gentle and lowly in heart, and you will find rest for your souls. For my yoke is easy, and my burden is light." Matthew 11:28-30

"I am the light of the world. Whoever follows me will not walk in darkness, but will have the light of life." John 8:12

"The thief comes only to steal and kill and destroy. I came that they may have life and have it abundantly. I am the good shepherd. The good shepherd lays down his life for the sheep." John 10:10-11

When you Feel Overwhelmed and Hopeless

- **Don't Panic:** Take a few deep breaths and tell someone what's troubling you.
- **Don't Let Go of <u>Invisible Hope</u>:** Though it seems there is no hope in regaining something or someone back, don't let go of **invisible hope**. Whatever the tragic situation, your life will turn for the better, give hope time to reappear. Be patient and ask for help. *Call on Christ, he is the savior of the hope-lost person, the Lord of the lonely inside, and the master rebuilder of life.*
- **Remind Yourself:** Life can be put together again. God still has a plan for your life, and He knows how to help you deal with your problems. It may seem impossible, and your life may seem to be in pieces—like Humpty Dumpty. God created us and he knows where every piece belongs, and the power to put them back to bring wholeness. Make the choice to allow him to restore you.

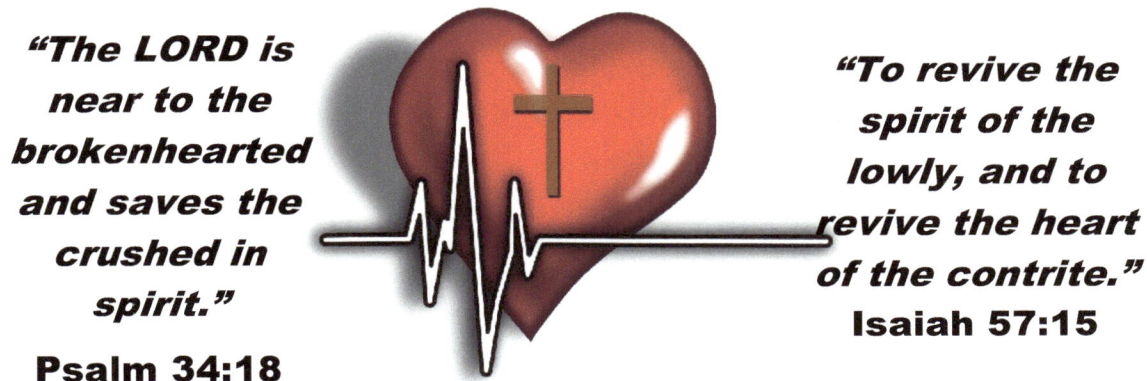

"The LORD is near to the brokenhearted and saves the crushed in spirit."
Psalm 34:18

"To revive the spirit of the lowly, and to revive the heart of the contrite."
Isaiah 57:15

Still Feel Like You are on the Edge?

1. **Tell someone in your support group or network how you feel.**
2. **Contact your emergency "go to" person:**

    Name: _____ Tel. No.: (_____) _____-_____
3. **Call the local crisis line: 719-275-2351**
4. **Can't stop thinking self-destructive thoughts, call: (800) 273-8255**

MCGM Recovery Through Christ Guidelines

- **Learn to make the most from a difficult situation:** You are in crisis and the living situation may be difficult. Being bitter about your situation won't help yourself or our efforts to help you but will most likely hinder and slow progress. Whatever the reason for your situation, find out why and make the best of your difficulty. Take this time to learn how to not repeat your cycles of trouble.
- **Teamwork with others in recovery and your facilitator:** You may be living in tight quarters and forced to share limited resources and basic living amenities. Keep a positive team work attitude and a hardy work ethic in sharing required duties and chores.
- **Personal Responsibilities:** You are encouraged to hold yourself accountable to daily routines: by maintaining specified rise and shine time; keeping up with personal hygiene; following a stable morning/evening routine; promptly doing chores; keeping your children safe and managed; keeping your appointments or calling if rescheduling is required; and learning to be patient with those helping you (as they have many duties). <u>Be courteous, thankful, and helpful.</u>
- **Courtesy and respect for others and other people's possessions:** If you are living in a shelter or group emergency housing. Keep track of your own personal property and use specified storage containers and respect your fellow guest's personal property.
- **Recovery rules:** Drugs and alcohol use and returning to your living quarters under the influence as well as prescribed medication overdosing may cause immediate eviction. Make sure you leave and return to your living quarters at designated times. Arguing, fighting, or inciting others to anger will put the instigator or perpetrator at risk of eviction.
- **Attend Monday Evening life skills classes:** Faithful attendance of the Jump Start Life Now—life skills class is vital. Classes are designed to help you work through your situation and help prevent reoccurring trouble in your life.
- **Dealing with a person who antagonizes or bullies:** Unfortunately, some people in you family or living situation may become emotional, contentious, and even combative. DO NOT try to defuse, confront, or correct. Immediately remove yourself the situation. If threatened call 911.
- **Connecting with the right resource:** Listed in this workbook are local resources available to help you to get back up and running on all cylinders. Your main goal is to patiently find the right help and stick with it. Your short-term goal is to stabilize your emotions and thoughts, then patiently and diligently solve your legal challenges if any, find work, and work towards finding a more permanent living arrangement. DO NOT HESTITATE TO ASK FOR HELP – but also do your part.

Community Resource List

Housing Assistance:

Loaves & Fishes Chayah House Shelter
241 Justice Center Rd. Canon City   719-275-0593
UAACOG Mutual Self Help Housing Program
3224-A Independence Rd. Canon City   719-275-8350
Habitat for Humanity
727 S. 8th St. Canon City   719-275-7781
Section 8 Housing
3224-A Independence Rd. Canon City   719-275-4979

SENIOR/ DISABLED Low-income and/or Subsidized Housing:

Canon Club Apartments – Jennifer Dingman
431 Macon Ave. Canon City   719-275-0219
Three Links Apartments – Jane Traxler
1300 N 15th St. Canon City   719-269-9134
Villa Canon Apartments – Kathi Lindsey
2400 E. Main St. Canon City   719-275-6410
Garden Park Villa Apartments – Lenore Garcia
1821 N. 5th St. Canon City   719-275-6656
Royal Gorge Manor * no accommodations for disabled* – Debbie Sims
1122 N. 15th St. Canon City   719-275-6545
San Juan Apartments – Jill Porterfield
1101 E. Main St. Florence   719-784-6914
<u>**Low- Income Housing (Single Individuals):**</u>
Villa Carina 431 Harrison Ave. Canon City   719-275-3519

Transitional Housing:

<u>**Restoring Hope Transitional Housing Program:**</u>

Restoring Hope is a six to twelve-month rapid rehousing program geared toward families. To qualify for the program, clients must be homeless and have children. Clients must adhere to program guidelines including but not limited to: attending weekly life skills classes, as well as participating in home visits with their case managers. Program openings are contingent on clients graduating from the program, and the waiting list varies in length of clients and time.

<u>**New Creations Inn Transitional Housing Program:**</u>

New Creations Inn is a one-year transitional housing program geared toward singles who are wishing to recover from addictions, and to any single person who is looking to make a positive change in their lives. This is a structured environment with weekly case management, community chores, devotionals, and community meals. NCI is located at the motel next door to the E-Free Church; this is where the residents stay. Program openings vary.

 Please Note: Applications for Restoring Hope and New Creations Inn may be picked up at the Loaves and Fishes main office; 241 Justice Center Rd. Canon City; Monday to Friday from 8am to 4pm. For questions, please call the main office at 719-275-0593 during normal business hours.

Transportation:

Senior Services Solutions Plus: 719-275-3900
Transport to MEDICAL & DENTAL APPTS. 321 N. Cottonwood Canon City
Round trip fees: $5 in town; $7 Florence, Penrose; $12 Pueblo; $17 CO Springs
If on Medicaid, fees may be waived but will need to be verified.
Must be over 18 years old to receive transport; transport Monday to Friday.
Note: DO NOT TRANSPORT WHEELCHAIRS.

Golden Age Shuttle/Fremont County Transit: 719-276-5200

Fremont Cab: 719-784-2222

Hank's Travel Plaza/ Mt. Goat Bus (Chaffee Shuttle): 719-276-8465

Pueblo Transit Center: Court & 1st Ave. Pueblo 719-553-2727

Greyhound Customer Service: 800-752-4841

Service Providers:

Fremont County Dept. of Human Services
172 Justice Center Rd. Canon City 719-275-2318

Sol Vista Health
3225 Independence Rd. Canon City 719-275-2351

Rocky Mountain Behavioral Health
3239 Independence Rd. Canon City 719-275-7650

Colorado Workforce Center
3224-B Independence Rd. Canon City 719-275-7408

UAACOG (Upper Arkansas Council of Governments)
3224-A Independence Rd. Canon City 719-275-8350

Center for Disabilities- Joseph Sims
105 N. 10th St. Canon City 719-251-5002
901 W. 8th St Pueblo 719-546-1271

Canon City Pregnancy Center
508 Greenwood Ave. Canon City 719-275-7074

Salvation Army Fremont County
Pat Trotta- Fremont County Director 719-371-0022

Fremont County Department of Public Health
201 N. 6th St. Canon City 719-276-7449

Legal Aide:

Fremont County Court
615 Macon Ave. Canon City 719-276-7410
Thursdays 9:30am, located in basement—first come, first serve basis

Services for Homeless Military Veterans:

Benjamin Strand (Veteran Support Specialist)
Rocky Mountain Human Services
Contact Benjamin Strand for details
17 S. Weber St. Colorado Springs, CO 719-649-2974

Crisis Intervention Services:

Fremont County Suicide Hotline	719-275-2351
Canon City Victims' Assistance	
161 Justice Center Rd. Canon City	719-276-5600
Fremont County Victims' Assistance	
100 Justice Center Rd. Canon City	719-276-5518
Safe2Tell	877-542-7233
American Red Cross	719-561-2614
Poison Control	800-222-1222
Pueblo Suicide Prevention Center Help Line	719-544-1133
National Suicide Prevention Lifeline	800-273-8255

Personal Support Network

Counselor

Name: _____ Tel. No.: (_____) _____-_____

Organization: _____

Fellowship Pastor/Mentor

Name: _____ Tel. No.: (_____) _____-_____

Organization: _____

Recovery Group Facilitator

Name: _____ Tel. No.: (_____) _____-_____

Organization: _____

Recovery Partner (Another likeminded believer working with you)

Name: _____ Tel. No.: (_____) _____-_____

Organization: _____

Emergency Contact Person

Name: _____ Tel. No.: (_____) _____-_____

Relationship to you: _____

Other Important Contacts:

Name: _____ Tel. No.: (_____) _____-_____

Name: _____ Tel. No.: (_____) _____-_____

Name: _____ Tel. No.: (_____) _____-_____

Name: _____ Tel. No.: (_____) _____-_____

Name: _____ Tel. No.: (_____) _____-_____

Jump Start Life Now

Class Topic No. 1: Restoring Hope

Date: ___/___/___   Speaker: _____

Share with the group....

- One thing that you are grateful for today.
- One accomplishment this week that helped in your recovery.
- One insight on <u>why</u> things went wrong and how to change the <u>why</u>.
- One thing you did to help someone else.

Quotes for the day:

Hope deferred makes the heart sick, but a desire fulfilled is a tree of life. Proverbs 13:12

Keep your heart with all vigilance, for from it flow the springs of life. Proverbs 4:23

The LORD is near to the brokenhearted and saves the crushed in spirit. Psalm 34:18

For thus says the One who is high and lifted up, who inhabits eternity, whose name is Holy: "I dwell in the high and holy place, and also with him who is of a contrite and lowly spirit, to revive the spirit of the lowly, and to revive the heart of the contrite. Isaiah 57:15

Class Discussion and Comments:

Hope: a feeling of expectation and desire for a certain thing to happen. Synonyms: aspiration, desire, wish, expectation, ambition, aim, goal, plan, design; dream, daydream, pipe dream

- Consider how and why life fell apart.
- Learn to discover hidden baggage that sabotage good efforts at making life work.
- Hopeless and bitter expectations within the secret heart destroys our "want to," and becomes self-fulfilling.
- Evil is real and whacks good people, especially when good people take the wrong path.
- Does God really care about you and your situation? Do people helping you really care?
- God revives the <u>lowly in spirit</u> and those of a <u>contrite heart</u>. Why are these conditions required by the Lord that we might receive his help?

Class Notes:

_____
_____
_____
_____
_____
_____
_____

Reigniting Your WANT TO?

"When Jesus saw him and knew that he had been lying there a long time, he said to him, "Do you want to be healed?" (John 5:6). Christ brings the same question to us, "Do you want to be made whole and have your life restored?"

In the case of this man, lying crippled for years, Christ commanded him to, *"Rise, take up your pallet and walk."* No matter the depth of our despair, if we believe in Christ and act on what little faith we have and take the first step in our recovery, the Lord will bless and help us as we continue taking each step.

Just as Christ knew about this man, He knows every reason and every wound within us that has crippled us spiritually and emotionally. Stir up your WANT TO by taking one step at a time.

Do what you know you can and should do and trust that God will take care of the rest. *"But be doers of the word, and not hearers only, deceiving yourselves… But the one who looks into the perfect law, the law of liberty, and perseveres, being no hearer who forgets but a doer who acts, he will be blessed in his doing.* (James 1:22-25)

Journal

_____
_____
_____
_____
_____
_____
_____
_____
_____
_____
_____
_____
_____
_____
_____
_____
_____
_____
_____
_____
_____
_____
_____

Jump Start Life Now

Class Topic No. 2: Receiving Help from Others

Date: ____/____/____   Speaker: _____

Share with the group....
- One thing that you are grateful for today.
- One accomplishment this week that helped in your recovery.
- One insight on <u>why</u> things went wrong and how to change the <u>why</u>.
- One thing you did to help someone else.

Quotes for the day:

"And when the Pharisees saw this, they said to his disciples, "Why does your teacher eat with tax collectors and sinners?" But when he heard it, he said, "Those who are well have no need of a physician, but those who are sick. Go and learn what this means, 'I desire mercy, and not sacrifice.' For I came not to call the righteous, but sinners" (Matthew 9:11-13).

The Parable of the Prodigal Son: *"But when he <u>came to himself</u>, he said, 'How many of my father's hired servants have more than enough bread, but I perish here with hunger! I will arise and go to my father, and I will say to him, "Father, I have sinned against heaven and before you."* Luke 15:17-18

Class Discussion and Comments:
- **Denial:** Pride keeps many struggling with instability and addictions, keeping us stuck in destructive cycles. Many live in habitual disassociation by justifying, minimizing, blaming, or rationalizing their addictions.
- **Pig Pen Therapy:** Life's troubles should help us break denial; by realizing what we are doing is not working, it should bring us to our senses and break our self-destructive pride. This allows for God to send help from someone outside our circumstance and help you reason out your situation—and to learn how to stop the cycle. Meaningful help usually comes from someone who also hit bottom and knows the ropes in overcoming and knows how to jump start life the right way.
- **Most are the Same Boat:** We must learn to not beat ourselves up because our wrong choices in life has finally caught up with us. Most people at one time or another have gone through some process of being forced to come to their senses, became humble and contrite, and learned to ask God for help.
- **Have You Hit Bottom Yet?** Are you broken of believing your OWN LIE? Are you broken enough to receive help from God through others and from God himself, to be healed and transformed on the inside?
- **Note:** The prodigal son's brother was jealous that his messed up, once wayward brother was received with open arms by their father. Many are driven into a troubled life as the black sheep of the family, programmed to fail from the subtle pressure from a smug sibling or family member. The self-righteous often attack the weaker out of jealousy and competition.

Class Notes:

_____
_____
_____
_____

Ask, Seek, and Knock!

"Ask, and it will be given you; seek, and you will find; knock, and it will be opened to you. For everyone who asks receives, and he who seeks finds, and to him who knocks it will be opened... If you then, who are evil, know how to give good gifts to your children, how much more will the heavenly Father give the Holy Spirit to those who ask him!" (Luke 11:9-13).

Ask, seek, and knock is part of our work. Our heavenly Father is faithful, but we must approach Him with persistence and in faith. He knows what we need before we ask, but nevertheless we must humbly ask—never stop asking, never stop seeking and never stop knocking.

Stay humble when in need, and especially when blessed, then God can and will answer in many ways; however, our pride of life can easily blind us to how God sends help. Jesus said that he came to save the wounded and lost sinner, the key is recognizing that we are all lost and in desperate need of being saved from ourselves as well as evil that is all around us.

We don't need to become religious to seek God, but rather come with the attitude of repentance with the realization no one can approach God on the bases of their own goodness. You don't have to straighten yourself out before approaching God. Just acknowledge to him and to yourself how messed up you are and ask him to save and transform you. Ask, seek and knock with a humble heart and see God's answers come.

Journal Date: ____/____/____

Jump Start Life Now

Class Topic No. 3: Managing "Our" Anger

Date: ___/___/___   Speaker: _____

Share with the group....

- One thing that you are grateful for today.

- One accomplishment this week that helped in your recovery.

- One insight on <u>why</u> things went wrong and how to change the <u>why</u>.

- One thing you did to help someone else.

Quotes for the day:

"Be angry and do not sin; do not let the sun go down on your anger, and give no opportunity to the devil."
Ephesians 4:26-27
"Fathers, do not provoke your children to anger, but bring them up in the discipline and instruction of the Lord."
Ephesians 6:4
"A gentle tongue is a tree of life, but perverseness in it breaks the spirit." Proverbs 15:4
"A glad heart makes a cheerful face, but by sorrow of heart the spirit is crushed." Proverbs 15:13
"A joyful heart is good medicine, but a crushed spirit dries up the bones." Proverbs 17:22

Class Discussion and Comments:

Unresolved anger smolders into pools of pent up rage. Like a time-bomb, pent up rage can be cued up through agitation, anxiety, or by an altercation and fear. The result is irrational thoughts and destructive actions. Unresolved anger from an abusive childhood is the primary root reason for people going ballistic.

Embracing the process of identifying (remembering) the trauma that created the unresolved anger is the first step in draining our pools of rage. The pain that caused the anger can be resolved with understanding—when we grasp the truth internally, complete resolution, recovery, and peace replaces inner turmoil and self-pity, anger, jealousy and a vindictive hard heart.

The process of releasing these internal issues is called catharsis, and is a key process used by the Holy Spirit to help heal damaged emotions and wounds to our personal spirit caused by past trauma, defilements, and difficult times.

Catharsis: The process of releasing, and thereby providing relief from, strong or repressed emotions.
synonyms: emotional release, relief, release, venting; purging, purgation, purification, cleansing; abreaction

Class Notes:

_____
_____
_____
_____
_____
_____
_____

Patient Endurance!

"An inheritance gotten hastily in the beginning will in the end not be blessed. Do not say, 'I will repay evil'; wait for the LORD, and he will help you" (Proverbs 20:21,22).

Healing and restoration that leads to wholeness on the inside does not happen overnight. Be patient and diligent in taking each step that your faith instills. Do the work of paying attention to your thoughts and feelings. Learn to identify truthfully what you are feeling and why. Often, to get at the original trauma and root issues, we must first deal with the layers of added issues from similar trauma and disappointments that have compiled through the years.

Resist becoming frustrated. Many want instant results and are easily misled by imposters who teach self-help quick-fix gimmicks that lead wounded and naïve people down rabbit trails—ending in heartache. Or the other popular approach of managing unresolved feeling is through prescribed medication that have detrimental side effects.

Medication can help minimize the internal issues of anxiety, depression, and obsessions. However, medication also masks the indicators that our inner being is broadcasting that are designed to point to the inner root issues that need healing and resolution.

It is God's plan to restore your inheritance that is in Christ, but the Holy Spirit knows which issue and what wound to address at their proper time. So, trust God and routinely call upon Him for help and insight as to why you are still emotionally and mentally troubled.

Journal Date: ____/____/____

_____
_____
_____
_____
_____
_____
_____
_____
_____
_____
_____
_____
_____
_____
_____
_____
_____
_____
_____

Jump Start Life Now

Class Topic No. 4: <u>Relationship Boundaries</u>

Date: ____/____/____ Speaker: _____

Share with the group....
- One thing that you are grateful for today.
- One accomplishment this week that helped in your recovery.
- One insight on <u>why</u> things went wrong and how to change the <u>why</u>.
- One thing you did to help someone else.

Quote for the day:

Relationships based on neediness will inevitably stifle the personal growth of one or both parties stuck in a codependent-addictive relationship. People stuck in neediness will most likely cause their significant relationships to end in destruction and at best become dysfunctional, and likely become combative.

Class Discussion and Comments:
- What does emotional accountability in relationship boundaries mean?
- Do you know who you are to yourself? (Reality, Fantasy, or a Combination)
    - Relationship boundaries are primarily derived by what role we played in our family of origin. Setting proper boundaries requires breaking your **family of origin spell** (covered in a later class).
- Do you worry about what people think of you? (Or do you not care?)
- Do you feel controlled in certain relationships?
- Do you find yourself feeling and acting different in certain relationships?
- Do you caretake people who are needy? (Run to their rescue at your own or others' expense).
- Do you use others as a "means to an end?"
- Do you let others abuse and use you? Do you have a propensity to let certain people enable you to fall off the wagon?
- How patient and understanding are you when others make mistakes?
- Learning to truthfully say "no," "yes," and "I don't know" helps maintain proper boundaries.
- Respect for others and having dignity (self-respect) are important keys to establishing proper relationship boundaries.

Relationship Shrikes: A person who gathers righteousness to themselves by pointing out the flaws in others or continuously points out how things could have been done better, all in the guise of helping.

Class Notes:

_____
_____
_____
_____
_____
_____

Distancing Self from Game Players and Avoiding Evil Doers

"They count it pleasure to revel in the daytime. They are blots and blemishes, reveling in their deceptions, while they feast with you. They have eyes full of adultery, insatiable for sin. They <u>entice unsteady souls</u>. They have hearts trained in greed. Accursed children! 2 Peter 2:13-14

It is uncanny how game players and evil doers undermine wounded and struggling people who desire to live right. Even family members can sabotage one's recovery by subtly aggravating unhealed wounds that undermine clear thinking.

Learning to maintain proper boundaries with people and taking courage to avoid altogether those bent on mischief and sin is vital to one's recovery.

Journal Date: ____/____/____

Jump Start Life Now 21

Class Topic No. 5: Recovery from a Wounded Spirit

Date: ___/___/___   Speaker: _____

Share with the group….

- **For this lesson, group sharing to be directed by the facilitator, depending on time.**

Quotes for the day: *"A gentle tongue is a tree of life, but perverseness in it breaks the spirit"* (Proverbs 15:4)
"A man's spirit will endure sickness, but a crushed spirit who can bear?" Proverbs 18:14

"And the tongue is a fire. The tongue is an unrighteous world among our members, staining the whole body, setting on fire the cycle of nature [1], and set on fire by hell" (James 3:6). [1] Or wheel of birth or the whole course of life.

"He heals the brokenhearted and binds up their wounds" (Psalm 147:3).

Class Discussion and Comments:

- Trauma, especially during childhood, whether physical, emotional, or a sexual defilement—wounds the spirit and stains the whole body (emotionally, mentally, and physically).
- These wounds and stains continue with us and become layered by more wounds and stains from abuses and defilements, along with our own sinful reactions and sinful behavior. Theses stains build upon each other like layers of scar tissue covering wounds that are still tender and painful.
- Hurtful words and parental acts of abandonment, absenteeism, and rejection can cause severe damage to one's personal spirit and damage emotions. This is part of the scar tissue build up and can be referred to as a hardened heart that suppresses healthy, normal emotions. Though, not as acute as physical or sexual, however, they still leave an <u>almost permanent</u> stain on the spirit, soul, and mind.
- The cycle of nature or wheel of birth means that words that traumatize create stains upon our nature causing abnormal development of inner character structures and create inner misbeliefs about self, others, God, and life in general.
- All manner of behavior and habits and even different personalities are developed to cope and suppress unresolved anger and feelings of inadequacy. All making it difficult to manage living.
- Pockets or pools of rage, hysteria, and extreme craving for self-centered nurturing lay in wait to be cued up during life's challenges, or when life becomes boring.
- Subtle parental "performed to be loved" pressure can create internal anxiety that drives unwanted feelings and wrong behavior.
- One's spirit can be wounded in the form of defilements: Perverted nurturing perpetrated through non-physically-abusive sexual molestation by a parent, older sibling, or a babysitter, stains and activates sexuality before we are mature enough to manage our sexuality in a heathy manner.
- Most people who suffer from panic disorders, dissociative disorders, and other mental/emotional disorders have their disorders rooted from past wounds (trauma) to their personal spirit.
- Demonic influences work on wounds that stained. Inner fires of rage and desires are stoked by demons. Satan can spiritually push a wounded, rage carrying person into insanity and irrational behavior.

Class Notes:

_____

_____

Overcoming the Effects of Trauma

"A man's spirit will endure sickness, but a crushed spirit who can bear?" Proverbs 18:14
"The LORD is near to the brokenhearted and saves the crushed in spirit." Psalm 34:18

Many suffer from a wounded and crushed (shattered) spirit. Few recovery programs and psychiatric treatments address wounds to the human spirit, yet trauma that penetrates to the spirit not only damages the heart (emotions) but also the mind, especially the unconscious mind.

Most unstable people do not realize that they suffer from past trauma that caused damage to their spirit and emotions. When we realize that we suffer from a wounded spirit and call on God to help us recover—the process of healing and wholeness can become much more effective.

However, recovery from a crushed spirit is not instant and it requires understanding and willingness to work with the Holy Spirit and God's principles of recovery. Layers of personalities, misbeliefs, and the fear of feeling unresolved pain must be dealt with—step by step.

In God's recovery process, past trauma can be revealed, catharized, fully resolved and healed in God's proper timing. This requires the comfort and leading of the Holy Spirit where understanding and cooperation is learned and practiced.

With our cooperation, the Holy Spirit can penetrate to the very core of our wounds and bring healing. *"He heals the brokenhearted and binds up their wounds"* (Psalm 147:3).

Journal Date: ____/____/____

Jump Start Life Now

Class Topic No. 6: Conflict Management

Date: ___/___/___   Speaker: _____

Share with the group....

- One insight on <u>why</u> things went wrong and how to change the <u>why</u>.
- One thing you did to help someone else.

Quote for the day:

"A soft answer turns away wrath, but a harsh word stirs up anger" (Prov. 15:1).

"A hot-tempered man stirs up strife, but he who is slow to anger quiets contention" (Prov. 15:18).

"Whoever corrects a scoffer gets himself abuse, and he who reproves a wicked man incurs injury" (Prov. 9:7)

Class Discussion and Comments:

- Learn to maintain safe boundaries and develop a threat recognition **mindset**.
    - EMOTIONALLY and MENTALLY maintain SAFE SURROUNDING AWARENESS
- Learn to apply the "**uncontentious**" NO in firmness. What does this mean to the group?
- Use of the "**guilt-free**" NO and learning to agree to disagree without bitterness or retaliation helps resolve conflict.
- Standing for "**what is right**," not "**who is right**" and using "**silence**" to mitigate anger escalation (do not use silence as a revenge tool to ignore or aggravate).
- Learn to manage relationship conflict through humility and respect.
- Proper conflict resolution requires that we overcome our own contentious projection. What does the term projection mean? (See **FEELINGS**.)
- Healing false responsibility helps to overcome "double-bind relationships."
- Avoid correcting one who scoffs at the truth, if not, you are asking for trouble.
- **FEELINGS:** The "**You make me feel syndrome.**"
    - Sort out and own your feelings, and lovingly hold others accountable to take ownership of their feelings.
    - Unresolved trauma from the past is often the source of bad feelings directed at someone now. This is called <u>projecting</u>, where anger and resentment towards someone from your past, (someone who hurt you in which the trauma is yet to be healed and forgiven). These unresolved wounds can be inflamed or cued up and released like a projectile towards another who you are now in conflict with—in an outburst hate, often towards a loved one.

Contentious definition: Disagree just to disagree, perverse, quarrelsome, irrational—a bitter-envious negative outlook on life. In other terms, someone who scoffs at truth and reason, who lives in inner turmoil.
Think about this: People trapped in internal strife from past trauma and issues often demand an answer that can never be given by another **in the now**.
If the other is unwilling to argue fairly and reasonably then: <u>**SHUT UP and WALK AWAY!**</u>
<u>**Importantly, learn to forgive from the heart!**</u> (However, forgiveness does not negate our responsibility to hold others accountable to change wrong behavior and bad attitudes, this we will cover in a later class.)

Class Notes: Use next page for class notes.

Skills and Principles that Help Manage Living While in Crisis

> **God sees everything.**
>
> ***Especially what we can't see or don't want to see within ourselves.***
>
> *"And before him no creature is hidden, but all are open and laid bare to the eyes of him with whom we have to do"* (Hebrews 4:13).
>
> When we choose to see what God sees hidden within us, we can count on Him to show us (step by step) our hidden issues and how they got there. However, when we cover up our internal eyes and ignore His wooing, promptings, and revelation concerning our internal issues—God is then forced to no longer protect us from the troubles that so easily befall us. This can cause pressing circumstances incited by the devil. This pressure will occur until we come back to God in humble cooperation.
>
> Then, if we continue ignoring our issues and life's warnings, eventually God will abandon us to powers of darkness until we finally wake up—this can be a terrible situation to fall into—many never recover but go over to the dark side of life for keeps.
>
> Some end up falling into the devil's blessings where their conscience is no longer operating. Many made shipwreck their faith by rejecting conscience. (See 1 Timothy 1:18-20.)

Journal Date: ____/____/____

Jump Start Life Now

Class Topic No. 7: Rational - Critical Thinking
Or Learning Wisdom and Reason

Date: ____/____/____ Speaker: _____

Share with the group....
- One thing that you are grateful for today.
- One accomplishment this week that helped in your recovery.
- One insight on <u>why</u> things went wrong and how to change the <u>why</u>.
- One thing you did to help someone else.

Quote for the day:

> *"The beginning of wisdom is this: Get wisdom, and whatever you get, get insight"* (Proverbs 4:7).

Class Discussion and Comments:

- Do you rely on others to do what you need to do for yourself? If so why?
    - Do you live in fear, and have feelings of inadequacy, and are afraid to make a mistake?
- Are you easily enlisted to do things for others, that they should be doing for themselves?
- How do we learn to think and reason out our thoughts for ourselves? If necessary, do we confer with another who is reliable? (A person who shares what we NEED to hear, not what we WANT to hear.)
- When we make decisions for ourselves, not relying others to tell us what to do, we learn from our mistakes and successes.
- Take personal ownership for making decisions that are timely and wise.
- Don't bite off more than you can chew, so take Dirty Harry's advice, "Know your own limitations."
- Do you make rash and compulsive decisions? Is your data faulty? Are you emotionally wearing it?
- Wisdom is learning that you can only change yourself and that you cannot change others.
- What will happen when you change a negative attitude or bitter expectation?
    - Proper perceptions and true information help make right decisions.
- Damaged emotions can skew the reasoning process where perceptions and information gathering skills lack truth and lose sight of reality.
    - Rash or compulsive behavior comes from wounds to the spirit and damaged emotions.
- Scams, flattery, and lies easily deceive the heart of naïve people, as well as those who are trapped in bitter jealousy, selfish ambition, and greed.

Class Notes:

_____
_____
_____
_____
_____

Foolish Ideas and Low Self-Esteem

"If you have been foolish, exalting yourself, or if you have been devising evil, put your hand on your mouth." Proverbs 30:32

If we allow the Holy Spirit to reveal to us what the word of God really means, we will begin to see our motives for doing crazy things and making absurd decisions that often lead to folly. How many times have you asked yourself—what led me to make a wrong choice, say the wrong thing, buy something that you did not need that ruined your credit?

You might have had some clues, but you were never able to correct the reasons for the feelings that override common sense. Avoid letting damaged emotions effect sound judgment and proper reasoning processes. Learn to stop talking yourself into foolish and devilish behavior. Stop talking and listen to your thoughts before acting. A foolish idea stems from low self-image. We do foolish and wrong things because our inmost self believes that is who we are—foolish, unworthy, no-good.

If allowed, God can reveal the inner reasons and ill beliefs that foster a low self-esteem that drive compulsive behavior and stupid-childish actions and fool hearty schemes and wrong decisions.

Journal Date: ____/____/____

_____
_____
_____
_____
_____
_____
_____
_____
_____
_____
_____
_____
_____
_____
_____
_____
_____
_____
_____
_____
_____
_____

Jump Start Life Now

Class Topic No. 8: Pain Suppression and Addictions

Date: ___/___/___ Speaker: _____

Share with the group....
- One thing that you are grateful for today.
- One accomplishment this week that helped in your recovery.
- One insight on <u>why</u> things went wrong and how to change the <u>why</u>.
- One thing you did to help someone else.

Quote for the day:

"May the God of hope fill you with all joy and peace in believing, so that by the power of the Holy Spirit you may abound in hope" Romans 15:13

Class Discussion and Comments:
- We live in a culture of pain suppression and dissociative disorders that are developed to avoid pain.
- Emotional pain and mental angst are God's warning signals, like the oil-light on your car.
- God's peace and joy is often overridden by pain of unhealed spiritual trauma, past defilements and damaged emotions.
- Drugs, alcohol, food, sex, relationships, self-medication, compulsive behavior are temporary pain suppressants that have debilitating side effects.
- Our spirit, soul, and body build up an immunity to pain suppressants, demanding larger doses.
- Physiological/Psychological addiction have withdrawal symptoms.
- Become committed to an effective recovery program and seek help and comfort from a Higher Power that is Real (God through Christ). (Draw near to God and He will draw near to you!)
- Our pain suppressants don't come close to providing the peace and joy that God does when we abide in Christ.
- The fruit (effect) of the Holy Spirit is: love, joy, peace, patience, kindness, goodness, faithfulness, gentleness, self-control.

Class Notes:

_____
_____
_____
_____
_____
_____
_____
_____
_____

Emotional and Spiritual Numbing

"Let your laughter turn to mourning and your joy to dejection" (James 4:9).

The improper use of alcohol and drugs is an obvious attempt to suppress inner hidden pain. Not so obvious are the many legitimate past times that become obsessive such as hobbies, entertainment, sports, relationships, and even church work.

Powerful emotional/spiritual numbing activities has swept through the American culture and even Christianity. In many sections of Christianity carnal, entertaining worship has become an activity that stirs the personal spirit to act as an anti-depressant.

False doctrines that produce carnal religious activity deceives Christians into thinking they are okay when they are not, Carnal worship is used to conjure up false peace and false joy.

Avoid these activities and let the Lord expose the hidden painful issues that addictions and dissociative behavior suppress, (alcohol, drug, sexual obsession, false worship, passivity and alternate personality creation).

Allow mourning to come when a past unhealed trauma is revealed. Let the Holy Spirit show you the truth about the pain you are feeling, weep (catharize) and seek understanding from the Lord and allow His comfort to minister and resolve hidden pain. It takes time, but God is faithful to help resolve the inner pain from past trauma permanently.

The Holy Spirit will reveal the truth as to what happened and how your insides were twisted with misbeliefs and/or wrong thinking (associated with the past trauma).

Jesus said, *"You will know the truth, and the truth will set you free."* (See John 8:31-32.) Further, David wrote in Psalm 51:6, *"Behold, thou desirest truth in the inward being; therefore teach me wisdom in my secret heart."*

Journal Date: ____/____/____

Jump Start Life Now

Class Topic No. 9: Effective Communication

Date: ____/____/____ Speaker: _____

Share with the group….
- One thing that you are grateful for today.
- One accomplishment this week that helped in your recovery.
- One insight on <u>why</u> things went wrong and how to change the <u>why</u>.
- One thing you did to help someone else.

Quote for the day:
Know this, my beloved brothers: let every person be quick to hear, slow to speak, slow to anger; James 1:19

Class Discussion and Comments:
- Wants versus Needs: Learning to tell the difference and how to properly prioritize needs.
- Can emotions skew reality and hinder proper expressions of wants and needs?
- Heathy emotions produce what? Damaged emotions produce what?
- Based on our discussion, how can we **express constructive criticism**?
  - Accusatory, condemning, demeaning: or critique that is framed caringly, suggestive, and reasonable—in a humble manner.
- Learn to listen to others and listen to yourself before speaking, answering, or commenting.
  - Learn to catch yourself when interrupting others during conversations.
  - How do we effectively manage the above principles in effective communication?
  - How does our body language come through to others?
  - How effective is silence during conflict or when trying to stress an important point?
- Speed talking and pushy self-assertion comes from a self-centered person who has low self-esteem and a need to control the uncontrollable.
- Learn to be firm in presenting what is right, but not overbearing and controlling.

Class Notes:

_____
_____
_____
_____
_____
_____
_____
_____
_____
_____

> **Thoughts reveal issues of heart.**
>
> *"For out of the heart come evil thoughts, murder, adultery, fornication, theft, false witness, slander"* (Matthew 15:19).
>
> Many are taught to blame the devil for evil thoughts. Jesus was clear concerning this issue. When we learn to catch random-ill thoughts before we speak or act, we can then allow ourselves time to contemplate what to say before sticking our foot in our mouth.
>
> Later we can ask God to show us why the unclean or unhealthy thought is still within our hearts. Then cleansing can begin by repenting and asking for help in getting to the roots of bitterness that leads to healing of the original wound or cleansing a defilement.
>
> You can expect a dream, a memory, or a significant revelation in scripture to come **in a momen**t to help reveal the root source of the bad attitude. Often, the root source is a past unhealed trauma or an aspect of your former manner of life that helped grow inner bitterness, resentments, or jealousy.
>
> Learn to journalize or record the thought, then give up justifying the ill attitude and repent. You can then expect God to give you an answer in due time as He orchestrates a healing moment and resolve the root wound.

Journal Date: ____/____/____

_____
_____
_____
_____
_____
_____
_____
_____
_____
_____
_____
_____
_____
_____
_____
_____
_____
_____
_____
_____

Jump Start Life Now

Class Topic No. 10: Rebuilding a Proper Self-Image

Date: ____/____/____ Speaker: _____

Share with the group….
- **For this lesson, group sharing to be directed by the facilitator, depending on time.**

Quote for the day: *"Keep your heart with all vigilance, for from it flow the springs of life."* Proverbs 4:23

"Behold, you delight in truth in the inward being, and you teach me wisdom in the secret heart." Psalm 51:6

Find out what YOUR secret heart believes about YOU?

Class Discussion and Comments:
- Negative thoughts about self are related to damaged emotions and reveal your true self-image. Grandiose unrealistic thoughts also indicate damaged emotions; however, they often represent an internal counterbalancing of a negative self-image.
- Wounded people tend to compensate for a poor self-image by artificially jacking up self-esteem, which often comes across as arrogant, know it all, over assertive, and insensitive.
- Other characteristics of a poor self-image are feelings of bitterness, jealousy, and self-pity.
- We must discover internal lies and misbeliefs that produce a poor self-image. These wrong beliefs also sabotage our opportunities, relationships, and life in general.
  - Learn how to allow God to shine the truth-light of your wrong inner beliefs concerning:
    ✓ **God** ✓ **Self** ✓ **Others** ✓ **and your General Outlook on Life**
- Mental gymnastics and religion attempt to remodel our self-image, only works to a point.
- Transforming the heart is Christ's work, if we choose to let Him by cooperating and following His ways!
- God has the power to correctly restore a poor self-image into a truthful non-negative and self-respectful internal outlook of self.
- We must learn to allow the Holy Spirit to show us our damaged emotions, wounds to our spirit, and our inner core self-beliefs that are wrong, so we can work with His love and grace to become changed on the inside.
- **Epiphany of Truth:** A manifestation of a truthful insight that is divinely revealed: a moment of sudden revelation or insight. A healing moment where the Holy Spirit brings real comfort to heal, cleanse, facilitate forgiveness. A moment of internal true enlightenment.
- For Christ said of his work: *"If you abide in my word, you are truly my disciples, and you will know the truth, and the truth will set you free"* John 8:31-32. Thus, in doing so, Christ will change our springs of life to become full of life and life giving, not life taking from others, and receiving God's blessings naturally without fuss, anxiety, and overworking.

"On the last day of the feast, the great day, Jesus stood up and cried out, 'If anyone thirsts, let him come to me and drink. Whoever believes in me, as the Scripture has said, <u>Out of his heart will flow rivers of living water</u>.'" John 7:37-38

Use opposite page journal section for Class Notes.

No More Self-Condemnation

"There is therefore now no condemnation for those who are in Christ Jesus. For the law of the Spirit of life in Christ Jesus has set me free from the law of sin and death. For God has done what the law, weakened by the flesh, could not do:" (Romans 8:1-3).

When a wounded Christian is overtaken by a sin, often self-condemning thoughts begin to scream within the mind and produce unrelenting mental and emotional torment. (On top of our own self-condemnation, the devil often injects subliminal thoughts through our spirit that fuels more self-condemning thoughts and creates more internal misery.)

Immediately, admit the sins as they occur, repent, and come to Christ seriously seeking forgiveness. Do not rationalize, justify, minimize, or blame another for what happened.

Then seek God to find the answer why you acted sinfully (provided you are not sinning deliberately) and you will be forgiven. God will show the reasons and administer grace, understanding, and healing. If we are honest with ourselves and honest with God, God will not condemn us; nor should we continue to condemn ourselves.

"If we confess our sins, he is faithful and just to forgive us our sins and to cleanse us from all unrighteousness" (1 John 1:9).

Be careful who you confess your sins to, many point a condemning finger religiously, having no mercy or grace to give support to others to help in recovery and be encouraged.

"Brethren, if a man is overtaken in any trespass, you who are spiritual should restore him in a spirit of gentleness. Look to yourself, lest you too be tempted. Bear one another's burdens, and so fulfil the law of Christ" (Galatians 6:1-2).

There is a definite difference between one who sins deliberately and one who is overtaken in a sin through temptation.

Journal Date: ____/____/____

Jump Start Life Now

Class Topic No. 11: God's Grace and Mercy

Date: ____/____/____ Speaker: _____

Share with the group....
- One thing that you are grateful for today.
- One accomplishment this week that helped in your recovery.
- One insight on <u>why</u> things went wrong and how to change the <u>why</u>.
- One thing you did to help someone else.

Quote for the day:

"Let us then with confidence draw near to the throne of grace, that we may receive mercy and find grace to help in time of need" (Hebrews 4:16)

Class Discussion and Comments:
- Does God really affect the lives of troubled people and intervene with His mercy and grace?
- How do we approach God to receive his intervening grace to help when we are in deep trouble?

God has made a way! The way is through His son Jesus Christ, with the following stipulations:
1) **Take Ownership:** We must stop blaming our failures and troubles that are due to a wayward life, on others or on the devil.
2) **Stop Self-Condemnation:** All of us make mistakes and do or have done sinful deeds. We must accept the reality that all people are prone to these things and stop condemning ourselves or compare ourselves to others.
3) **Renounce Living in Self-Pity:** We often minimize, rationalize, justify, blame others, and even blame God, thinking He handed us a raw deal. We easily turn bitter when we see others get away with wickedness while they live the **High-Life** [1] What's worse, we often turn to evil to get even with others who do evil or to stop evil coming against us.
4) **Turn Away from a Sinful Life-style:** Become determined to walk with the Lord, not religiously, but as someone who wants to become changed on the inside by the Lord.
5) **Draw Near to God Humbly:** Privately, in your own words talk to your heavenly Father with sincerity and admitting your failures, problems and your needs, asking Him to forgive, and then confidently asking for his help, direction, provision, and intervention.
6) **Repeat steps 1-4:** Continue your walk with God through Christ by humbly approaching God for his grace and mercy. Learn to pay attention to the many blessings and answers to prayer as He guides you through life. And always be willing to admit your transgressions and seriously turn away from acting out sinfulness.

Class Notes:

_____
_____
_____

---

[1] **The Wicked High-Lifer:** Their plight is much worse than sinners who get into trouble. The high-lifers who do evil, who seem to be blessed, will in the end have their blessings drag them down into the pit with no remedy to be found. See James 5:1-6.

Turning over a new leaf?

"For godly grief produces a repentance that leads to salvation without regret, whereas worldly grief produces death" (2 Corinthians 7:10).

When living wrong catches up with people, many turn to others for help. Most people initially turn to those who feel sorry for them and are willing to give a handout and even a new start. The new start taken is like *turning over a new leaf*, an expression that means to start behaving in a different way and start living a better life-style.

Unfortunately, only few can succeed by just choosing to change their life-style. Most who turn over a new leaf still carry the inner twisted issues deep within. These undealt-with issues sabotage good efforts of making the changes required that straightens out life and stops the cycles of self-destruction.

What's missing for most who turn over a new leaf? A true sense of heart felt grief over the miserable chosen life-style. Or healing of past trauma that wounded one's personal spirit and damaged emotions that causes a broken and hardened heart.

A true godly grief, when achieved internally will produce real inner change of heart. When one reaches bottom and truly realizes that their heart needs an overhaul, and chooses to give up destructive behaviors, addictions, and a self-pitied outlook on life—recovery (salvation) takes hold. The result of godly grieving leaves no room in the heart for self-pity and bitter regrets or jealousies and spitefulness.

Turning over a new leaf without heart felt grief and repentance sooner than later leads a wounded person back to a worse condition than before. However, when we continue to move forward with a heartfelt humble grief over our inner sour issues, then God's grace and mercy continues to facilitate the healing of our broken heart and wounded spirit—life becomes blessed.

Journal Date: ____/____/____

_____
_____
_____
_____
_____
_____
_____
_____
_____
_____
_____
_____
_____
_____
_____
_____

Jump Start Life Now

Class Topic No. 12: <u>Proper Prospective of Life</u>

Date: ____/____/____ Speaker: _____

Share with the group....
- One thing that you are grateful for today.
- One accomplishment this week that helped in your recovery.
- One insight on <u>why</u> things went wrong and how to change the <u>why</u>.
- One thing you did to help someone else.

Quote for the day:
"The fear of the LORD is the beginning of wisdom; all those who practice it have a good understanding."
                                                                                                        Psalm 111:10.
Do not be deceived: God is not mocked, for whatever one sows, that will he also reap." Galatians 6:7

Class Discussion and Comments:
- Leaning proper life skills requires a good understanding of how life on earth flows.
  - Anvils fall from the sky indiscriminately for those who tread the wrong path in life.
- Humility and proper respect for life's pitfalls will help restore hope and direction.
- NO FEAR mindset may seem to work; however, the truth is we are "not at all" **invisible or invincible.**
- Choosing to numb anxieties from the problems of life makes life's problems overwhelming in the end.
- Learn to keep your mouth shut, follow directions, and submit to authority.
  - Don't learn this lesson the hard way. (Group can give personal examples.)
- It takes courage to stay humble, yet do not become a doormat or a suck-up.
- Walking in the fear of the Lord helps navigate through life's minefields. He will guide you out of harm's way and deliver you from your enemies (if you follow Him).
- Know your limitations and learn to gain knowledge and understanding in everyday living, in work, within relationships, and how to walk through an open door (take advantage of a valid opportunity).
- The powers of darkness and evil prey on those who lack knowledge and truth and thumb their nose at God, having a NO FEAR attitude. (Those having NO FEAR evolves into becoming arrogant and taking foolish risks.)

Troubles in this world should lead us to our Savior, for our Lord said concerning his teachings:
"I have said these things to you, that in me you may have peace. In the world you will have tribulation. But take heart; I have overcome the world." John 16:33

Class Notes:

_____

_____

_____

A Broken or Wounded Conscious?
Sinning Deliberately? There is no free pass!

"For if we sin deliberately after receiving the knowledge of the truth, there no longer remains a sacrifice for sins, but a fearful prospect of judgment, and a fury of fire which will consume the adversaries" (Hebrews 10:26-27).

Do not be deceived; when we sin deliberately, we put ourselves in jeopardy. Break the habit of sinning deliberately, for when we sin on purpose, we remove ourselves from God's protection, grace, and mercy.

The devil is constantly looking for another "runaway child of God," usually a person in self-pity, bitterness, and rebellion—who turns to evil to fight evil.

When we sin deliberately, especially as a Christian, we end up rejecting our conscious (our internal warning system given to us by God). Doing this long enough will make our conscience broken.

If we keep sinning deliberately, we can run the risk of wrecking our faith and belief in God entirely. *"This charge I entrust to you, Timothy, my child, in accordance with the prophecies previously made about you, that by them you may wage the good warfare, <u>holding faith and a good conscience. By rejecting this, some have made shipwreck of their faith.</u>"* (1 Timothy 1:18-19).

However, on the other side of the coin, many are overtaken by sin and beat themselves unmercifully. Their conscious is wounded and often a nearby self-righteous hypocrite condemns, shames, and shuns those who are overtaken by the least wrongdoing.

"Brothers, if anyone is caught in any transgression, you who are spiritual should restore him in a spirit of gentleness. Keep watch on yourself, lest you too be tempted. Bear one another's burdens, and so fulfill the law of Christ" (Galatians 6:1-2).

Journal Date: ____/____/____

Jump Start Life Now

Class Topic No. 13: <u>Stress Management</u>

Date: ___/___/___ Speaker: _____

Share with the group....
- One thing that you are grateful for today.
- One accomplishment this week that helped in your recovery.
- One insight on <u>why</u> things went wrong and how to change the <u>why</u>.
- One thing you did to help someone else.

Quotes for the day:

"Casting all your anxieties on him, because he cares for you" (1 Peter 5:7).

"But understand this, that in the last days there will come times of stress. For men will be lovers of self, lovers of money, proud, arrogant, abusive, disobedient to their parents, ungrateful, unholy, inhuman, implacable, slanderers, profligates, fierce, haters of good, treacherous, reckless, swollen with conceit, lovers of pleasure rather than lovers of God, holding the form of religion but denying the power of it. Avoid such people" (2 Timothy 3:1-5).

Class Discussion and Comments:
- Perform to be loved and accepted, and having a shame based self-image—are built in stressors.
- Are you trying to control the uncontrollable?
- Are you internally comparing yourself to others and either feeling superior or inadequate?
- Who do you let stress you? Who are you competing against for recognition, and who is it that you are trying to impress?
- Stop ignoring stress, but recognize it and then work with God to resolve stress triggers by:
  - Healing past trauma that instilled pools of rage, fears, insecurities, and self-loathing.
- Casting your anxieties upon God – is not a magic mantra.
  - This requires submitting your life to God and putting your trust in Him.
  - Casting means letting God know in prayer how anxious you really are and become willing to let God show you your hidden issues of unbelief within your heart (and secret heart). Unbelief within the heart is basically not trusting God for help in time of need. This leads to an internal struggle of stress that leads to unconscious worry in trying to control the uncontrollable.

Class Notes:

_____
_____
_____
_____
_____
_____
_____

Overcoming Shame Based Living.

"...looking to Jesus the pioneer and perfecter of our faith, who for the joy that was set before him endured the cross, despising the shame" (Hebrews 12:3).

Wounded Christians invariably carry imposed shame from their past. It appears as self-condemnation when a mistake is made or where other people express rejection or disapproval.

Usually a shamed based wounded Christian is in constant internal angst and worry about what others think of them, or if others like them—and often perceive the worst in life, even though the opposite is true. Often, inner voices of self-condemnation become almost unbearable. Inner beliefs and inner personalities perceive any mistake as a sin and abhorred failure.

It was Satan working through evil people that imposed a shameful death upon Christ, but he despised that imposed shame from those who cried "crucify him."

Our Lord did not allow himself to absorb their projected shame, but rather detested the shame. His life and sacrifice on the cross and resurrection allows repentant sinners like you and I to be able to approach God without shame or condemnation.

So, to, we must despise our own self-imposed shame still emanating from our old-self and wounded-divided parts.

We will begin to overcome worrying about what others may or may not think about us. *"Let us then with confidence draw near to the throne of grace, that we may receive mercy and find grace to help in time of need"* (Hebrews 4:16).

Journal Date: ____/____/____

_____
_____
_____
_____
_____
_____
_____
_____
_____
_____
_____
_____
_____
_____
_____
_____
_____
_____

Jump Start Life Now

Class Topic No. 14: Overcoming Learning Disabilities

Date: ___/___/___   Speaker: _____

Share with the group….

- One thing that you are grateful for today.
- One accomplishment this week that helped in your recovery.
- One insight on <u>why</u> things went wrong and how to change the <u>why</u>.
- One thing you did to help someone else.

Quote for the day:

"He heals the brokenhearted and binds up their wounds" (Psalm 147:3).

Most learning disabilities stem from childhood issues, where lack of proper nurturing along with emotional, mental, and physical trauma produced wounds to the personal spirit and damaged emotions (a broken and hardened heart). Family of origin dysfunctionality creates a passive spirit that shrinks back from engaging in normal mental development. Instead, wounded people tend to develop dissociative disorders that short circuit normal development of mental abilities to problem solving and comprehend abstract ideas and think clearly.

Class Discussion and Comments:
- Lack of parental nurturing and proper guidance thwarts eagerness to learn.
- The TV baby sitter is a form of parental rejection and absenteeism and helps induce a passive approach to life's challenges, creating lethargy, lack of motivation, or a freeze or flee approach to learning.
- God can heal our passivity and restore our confidence to learn.
- When healed of our spiritual passivity, study and learning becomes a joy instead of drudgery and fearfully loathed.

Class Notes:

_____
_____
_____
_____
_____
_____
_____
_____
_____
_____

Truth in the inward being.

"Behold, thou desirest <u>truth in the inward being</u>; therefore, teach me wisdom in my <u>secret heart</u>" (Psalm 51:6).

People wounded in spirit develop various coping mechanisms, one most common is pretending, which is a form of denial.

Those who are wounded learn to turn their imagination into an internal make-believe system where truth is watered down or completely rewritten. Internally these make-believe lies become truth for people steeped in denial, as they act out what they believe.

Therefore, our denial of past pain and trauma becomes strong. As children, we learn to pretend pain away by creating an alternate scenario to believe.

Fantasy becomes an escape mechanism that invades rational thinking. When we come to God, it is truth about ourselves and our past, and its effects upon us now that must be restored in the inward being.

Learn to love and embrace truth on the inside, in your secret heart. Then our misbeliefs and unbelief can be transformed into inner truth that enables us to stand and move through our everyday challenges of life successfully.

Journal Date: ____/____/____

Jump Start Life Now

Class Topic No. 15: Identifying the Trouble Maker

Date: ____/____/____   Speaker: _____

Share with the group....
- One thing that you are grateful for today.
- One accomplishment this week that helped in your recovery.
- One insight on <u>why</u> things went wrong and how to change the <u>why</u>.
- One thing you did to help someone else.

Quote for the day:

The Lord knows how to rescue the godly from trials, and to keep the unrighteous under punishment until the day of judgment, and especially those who indulge in the lust of defiling passion and despise authority. 2 Peter 2:9-10

I appeal to you, brothers, to watch out for those who cause divisions and create obstacles contrary to the doctrine that you have been taught; <u>avoid them</u>. For such persons do not serve our Lord Christ, but their own appetites, and by smooth talk and flattery <u>they deceive the hearts of the naive</u>. For your obedience is known to all, so that I rejoice over you, but I want you to be <u>wise as to what is good and innocent as to what is evil</u>. The God of peace will soon crush Satan under your feet. The grace of our Lord Jesus Christ be with you. Romans 16:17-20

Class Discussion and Comments:
- Certain people in life have gone to the dark side and naturally cause trouble for others.
    - Are there evil men and women in your life now or in the past who instigate trouble?
- Some are obvious while others who are evil, hide in a cloak of decency.
- Most evil who pretend to be good, do so to deceive the hearts of naïve people.
- Overcoming our own bent towards evil will help us detect and avoid the trouble maker.
- Many continue to be burned by evil people and never wise up. Learn to wise up now and realize that you need to discern evil and avoid evil.
- These people may straighten up when they hit bottom—they are usually rebel rousers, wanting to amass a posse' to follow them. Learn to avoid such people. The required severity of life's troubles to help such a person wake up, will have a ripple effect. More than often, their close friends are taken out too. Learn to stay clear lest, when they go down, you go down with them.

Class Notes:

_____
_____
_____
_____
_____

Avoid such people!

"I appeal to you, brethren, to take note of those who create dissensions and difficulties, in opposition to the doctrine which you have been taught; <u>avoid them</u>. For such persons do not serve our Lord Christ, but their own appetites, and by fair and flattering words they deceive the hearts of the simple-minded" (Romans 16:17, 18).

One characteristic of a wounded Christian is naiveté, where evil people and false brethren find wounded Christians easy prey.

A very important aspect of recovery is learning to discern so called Christian who deceives. Many are very good at deceiving because they are self-deceived, believing their own lie, thus becoming very convincing.

When learning to avoid a deceitful person, be prepared to be attacked, berated, and be victimized by malicious gossip. The Apostle wrote about the last times as becoming filled with evil people and phonies: *"Indeed, all who desire to live a godly life in Christ Jesus will be persecuted, while <u>evil people and impostors</u> will go on from bad to worse, <u>deceiving and being deceived</u>."* 2 Timothy 3:12-13

The devil's most insidious (crafty) work, is using evil people who appear to good. Take note of those cause trouble and avoid such people!

Journal Date: ____/____/____

Jump Start Life Now

Class Topic No. 16: Beware of Ooey-Gooey Evil

Date: ____/____/____   Speaker: _____

Share with the group....
- One thing that you are grateful for today.
- One accomplishment this week that helped in your recovery.
- One insight on why things went wrong and how to change the why.
- One thing you did to help someone else.

Quote for the day:
"They have eyes full of adultery, insatiable for sin. They entice unsteady souls. They have hearts trained in greed. Accursed children!" (2 Peter 2:14)

Class Discussion and Comments:
- There are people who learn to practice Ooey-Gooey evil. They purposely prey on vulnerable people who are all too eager to have friends who seem to have it together.
- These evil people deliberately use flattery to gain advantage over the naïve to control and manipulate.
- This kind of good evil hides in church and gathers naïve people to become their followers. These make themselves look like they are respected, knowledgeable, and pure as the driven snow.
- Many are religious and yet practice sin secretly, enticing weak believers into doing sinful acts. This type of person has rejected conscience and has most likely fallen completely into darkness.
- They are full of bitter jealousy and greed that is covered by charm and religiosity. They promise a quick solution to personal problems, but in the end, they fall way short in helping their victims—in the end they take the life and faith away from others in a very insidious (sneaky) way.
- These lie habitually and come to believe their own lie, and thus become very convincing.
- Jesus confronted this type of religious phony in his day by saying that they were like their father the devil who was a murderer and a liar, who has no truth in him. Jesus also said of these phony religious people that they looked good on the outside but were filthy, greedy, and perverse on the inside. (See John 8;44-47 and Matthew 23:13-36.)

Class Notes:

_____
_____
_____
_____
_____

The <u>evil-evil</u> hides in a cloak of decency

"Satan disguises himself as an angel of light. So it is no surprise if his servants, also, disguise themselves as servants of righteousness" (2 Corinthians 11:14-15).

The most insidious evil comes in the form of goodness and a helping hand, often using flattery to get the control and the upper hand in relationships. The undiscerning and naïve fall victim to these wolves disguised as sheep.

Many wounded people including wounded and naïve Christians succumb to oppression and even depression, not realizing that the source of their calamities is an evil person involved in their life. These **evil-evil** channel the devil's influence spiritually where feelings of oppressive, sicknesses, and even weird accidents befall their victims. Those attacked virtually have no clue as who the perpetrator is—a evil person who looks good but channels harmful invisible powers.

Even in ones extended family: an overbearing father, a self-righteous mother, a caretaking aunt or uncle who needs the extended family to remain needy and dependent upon them—will unconsciously and spiritually sabotage the wellbeing of others in their orbit of influence.

Wounded people often become influenced to do evil by a close friend who is a sycophant or a "Ooey-Gooey" suck-up who entices others to do evil.

Jesus referred to the Pharisees and the other phony religious leaders in his day as having the devil as their father. *"You are of your father the devil, and your will is to do your father's desires. He was a murderer from the beginning, and does not stand in the truth, because there is no truth in him. When he lies, he speaks out of his own character, for he is a liar and the father of lies"* (John 8:44).

Journal Date: ____/____/____

Jump Start Life Now

Class Topic No. 17: Breaking the Family of Origin Spell

Date: ___/___/___ Speaker: _____

Share with the group….
- **For this lesson, group sharing to be directed by the facilitator, depending on time.**

Quote for the day:

"If anyone comes to me and does not <u>hate</u> his own father and mother and wife and children and brothers and sisters, yes, and <u>even his own life</u>, he cannot be my disciple" Luke 14:26.

"The LORD is slow to anger and abounding in steadfast love, forgiving iniquity and transgression, but he will by no means <u>clear the guilty</u>, visiting the iniquity of the fathers on the children, to the third and the fourth generation." Numbers 14:18.

Class Discussion and Comments:
- The operative words in these two quotes will help make sense of seemingly crazy principles laid out by the Lord. They are "clear the guilty" and "even his own life." In the Luke passage, the word life in Christ's teaching in the original language means the carnal soulish life that is selfish and destructive. Dysfunctional families tend to control off springs and perpetuate a spell over family members, smothering members to miss out on becoming their own person.
- In the passage from Numbers, the warning is that sins, secret sins, and dysfunctionality are handed down to the next generation because the parents become and remain <u>guilty</u> of practicing sin and abuse. Not seeking repentance, confession, correcting, and not seeking forgiveness or making restitution—a similar pattern or propensity is handed down to their children to fall into similar sins and dysfunctionalities—which is passed on further to the third and the fourth generation.
- There is spell involved where the next generation is hard pressed to see the patterns. We refer to the family of origin spell as a <u>mutated replication of the family of origin system of abuse and dysfunctionality</u>.
- Dysfunctional and troubled people primarily suffer from unhealthy ties to their family of origin. Victims of the family of origin spell fall into false responsibility, a shame orientation and develop a "performed to be loved" internal drive. They learn to accept inner angst, suffer low self-esteem, and often as adults draw a co-dependent life from parents, siblings, or significant others.
- Those under the family spell have difficulty in finding their proper internal self-identification. They never become their own person, but falter through life trying to find out who they are in an endless internal search.
- Toxic family systems have shame based parenting that tends to enable and even push adult children towards sinning and living a dysfunctional-destructive life style. *Discuss shame based family system*.
- When we seriously follow Christ, the Lord will lead us away from this sick family of origin spell. He will press us to establish proper boundaries with our extended family. This will help us recovery the lost life due to these handed down generational traits.
- We must first learn to detect the many aspects of the family spell and <u>learn to hate it</u> so we can disconnect in a lovingly manner. However, most family leaders who love to perpetuate the family spell will resist breaking sick family ties tooth and nail, which can make the break a difficult battle.

Take Notes on next page.

Temporary Isolation Therapy

"Therefore, behold, I will allure her, and bring her into the wilderness, and speak tenderly to her. And there I will give her her vineyards, and make the Valley of Achor a door of hope" (Hosea 2:14, 15).

God leads his wounded into a period of isolation, where friends, family, and circumstances become strained and challenging. We use relationships to suppress our glaring issues and hide our own character flaws, thus God is required to lead us into a time of isolation.

This wilderness type period forces us to examine our own ways and brings us into intimacy with the Lord. In this type of Holy Spirit led therapy, God helps us to give up the gods (people) we so readily worship (often unconsciously). It is the toxic bad company that helps undermine our desire and efforts to walk right in life. The friends and loving family members we thought were helping turn out to actually be part of our demise in successful living.

It is these people who are enablers, controllers, manipulators, life drainers, who often undermine our progress with God and His recovery work.

Some even learn use spiritual powers to control thoughts, manipulate, harass, and cue up internal issues within their victims. These toxic people garner evil spiritual powers by actually seeking evil powers or indirectly through their own *hate ridden bitter jealous motives and wishful thinking.*

Journal Date: ____/____/____

_____
_____
_____
_____
_____
_____
_____
_____
_____
_____
_____
_____
_____
_____
_____
_____
_____
_____
_____

Jump Start Life Now 47

Class Topic No. 18: Disturbing Thought Catching

Date: ___/___/___ Speaker: _____

Share with the group....
- One thing that you are grateful for today.
- One accomplishment this week that helped in your recovery.
- One insight on <u>why</u> things went wrong and how to change the <u>why</u>.
- One thing you did to help someone else.

Quote for the day:

"But what comes out of the mouth proceeds from the heart, and this defiles a person. For out of the heart come evil thoughts, murder, adultery, sexual immorality, theft, false witness, slander. These are what defile a person. But to eat with unwashed hands does not defile anyone." Matthew 15:18-20

"Put off your old self, which belongs to your former manner of life and is corrupt through deceitful desires, <u>and to be renewed in the spirit of your minds</u>, and to put on the new self, created after the likeness of God in true righteousness and holiness. Ephesians 4:22-24

Class Discussion and Comments:
- Learn to slow down and catch your thoughts before acting upon them.
- Learn to distinguish the difference between normal self-talk within normal thinking and that of spontaneous thoughts that are sporadic, obsessive, weird, angry, impulsive and compulsive.
- Thoughts from our unconscious mind are strong indicators of issues, wounds, and defilements within our heart and spirit, where the spirit of the mind (unconscious mind) relays these inner issues to our conscious awareness.
- Don't freak out and think you are going crazy. Spontaneous thoughts, as are dreams and abnormal feelings, are major indicators given to us by the Lord. They inform us and warn us of issues that need to be addressed within our heart, spirit, and the spirit of mind (unconscious mind).

Class Notes:

_____
_____
_____
_____
_____
_____
_____
_____
_____

> **The gunk in others brings out the gunk in us.**
>
> *"A soft answer turns away wrath, but a harsh word stirs up anger"* (Proverbs 15:1).
>
> How do we react to harsh words? Do we tend to have stoked arguments with loved ones and blame the other for their mistakes, while minimizing, rationalizing, and justifying our own?
>
> How we react to the mistakes and failings of others indicates or points out our own condition of heart. Take ownership of your own sinful reactions to the sins and failings of others and determine to work with the Lord to trace down the root issues within your own heart.
>
> The blame game in relationships can become very destructive. Be angry but do not sin—take heed, lest you be consumed by each other (See Galatians 5:15). Remember Christ's teaching on judging others and the log in the eye analogy. (See Matthew 7:1-**5)**.
>
> Deal with roots of bitterness before they explode and hurt others. *"See to it that no one fails to obtain the grace of God; that no "root of bitterness" springs up and causes trouble, and by it many become defiled"* (Hebrews 12:15).

Journal Date: ____/____/____

Jump Start Life Now 49

Class Topic No. 19: Overcoming Escapism

Date: ___/___/___ Speaker: _____

Share with the group....
- One thing that you are grateful for today.
- One accomplishment this week that helped in your recovery.
- One insight on <u>why</u> things went wrong and how to change the <u>why</u>.
- One thing you did to help someone else.

Quote for the day:

Childhood abuse and neglect traumatizes our spirit, damages our emotions, and twists our thinking. The results are stains and scars in the form of inner emotional, mental, spiritual pain that effects our life, even as adults. Pretending the original pain away is a child's main coping mechanism, which requires the imagination to create an alternate reality. (A child can make-believe an alternate reality to become true internally—which is a form of disassociation.) Often self-induced amnesia is also automatically incorporated into the process of disassociation. The alternate or varied memory of the trauma is used to help deny the painful truth, often in total forgetfulness.

This somewhat works until we meet the reality of adulthood, where the unresolved pain grinds against challenges of adulthood, making life NOT work properly.

Adult escapism takes the place of childish pretending, where alcohol, drugs, sex, relationships, obsessive behavior, and the entertainment industry helps suppress the pain emanating from the inner stains and scars. The eventual side effects of escapism are more painful than embracing the truth concerning past suppressed childhood trauma.

Class Discussion and Comments:
- Why is it hard to grow up and put off childish-destructive behaviors?
- Alternate reality often produces alternate personalities whose job is to maintain pain relief and guard against further wounds.
- This process of pretending and escapism enslaves our lives to fun and selfishness that easily leads adult victims of childhood trauma into the darker side of life.
- What did Jesus say concerning knowing the truth?

Class Notes:

_____
_____
_____
_____
_____
_____
_____

Pretending, Imagination, or Inspiration

"And you will know the truth, and the truth will set you free" (John 8:32)

Learning to pretend reality away requires us to force our imagination to visualize an alternative and then try to create what we imagined or mimic what we see others do who seem to be happy. Thus, we fabricate an outer persona, or create alternate personalities to cope with life and suppress the pain held within the real inner person.

Jesus comes to help heal the real person within and transform the outer fabricated personas into healthy character and integrate healed and transformed personas or personalities into the very core of the person. This inner character and personality transformation is by the Holy Spirit. The new character formed is modeled and shaped to be like Christ's character and attitudes. *"And we all, with unveiled face, beholding the glory of the Lord, are being transformed into the same image from one degree of glory to another. For this comes from the Lord who is the Spirit"* (2 Corinthians 3:18).

The challenge is to allow the Lord to remove our blinders so we can realize the need for inner change and allow the Lord to transform us his way, not by religious hypocrisy, false spiritualism or magic thinking through pretending.

Then, from within, our transformed inner character will flow <u>true inspiration</u> and stability that overcomes life challenges.

"That according to the riches of his glory he may grant you to be <u>strengthened with power through his Spirit in your inner being</u>" (Ephesians 3:16).

Journal Date: ____/____/____

Jump Start Life Now

Class Topic No. 20: Activating Desire to Mature

Date: ____/____/____   Speaker: _____

Share with the group....
- One thing that you are grateful for today.
- One accomplishment this week that helped in your recovery.
- One insight on <u>why</u> things went wrong and how to change the <u>why</u>.
- One thing you did to help someone else.

Quote for the day:

Many stay immature as adults because of the loss of a healthy and maturing childhood. Aspirations of growing in knowledge, wisdom, and character became retarded and for some, their ambitions become dead. Many who are wounded live in a zombie-like-state, with the belief, "That's all there is to life." Few in this condition see any type of future, until they hear the truth.

Once we know the truth about what happened and how we can recovery, it is up to us to reactivate the desire to grow up, by continually learning. Then we can be counted upon as examples of inspiration to our family, friends, and others we meet in everyday life. God, through Christ can restore the right kind of aspirations if we allow Him to grow us into maturity.

Class Discussion and Comments:
- We must activate the desire to restore our "want to." We must stop floating along from event to event, thinking that life is short, so have fun and do our own thing.
- Many suffer a lost childhood and as adults live childishly, having adult toys to play with. This mindset squelches the desire to mature, where we unconsciously try to live out our lost childhood dreams. Most have a difficult time understanding the inner motives that drive obsessive childish behavior and habits.
- Many wounded people suffer from a slumbering spirit and passively stumble through life.
- Christ can, if asked and allowed to work inside us, break passivity and restore our desire to mature.

Class Notes:

_____
_____
_____
_____
_____
_____
_____
_____
_____

Wake up and grow up

"But when anything is exposed by the light, it becomes visible, for anything that becomes visible is light. Therefore it says, "Awake, O sleeper, and arise from the dead, and Christ will shine on you." Look carefully then how you walk, not as unwise but as wise, making the best use of the time, because the days are evil" (Ephesians 5:13-16).

Wounded people, including wounded Christians suffer from hidden issues within their heart and spirit. The devil uses unhealed wounds from past trauma to bring oppression and sabotage good efforts in living successfully.

One of the characteristics of being wounded is apathy and passivity. Many wounded prefer to stay asleep concerning these hidden issues, some in this condition live in a near zombie-like state. That is why alcohol, drug abuse, and sexual obsession is at epidemic levels. These harmful activities are used by wounded people to stay asleep and to numb the inner turmoil, emotional instability, and mental angst.

One of the works of the Holy Spirit is to activate the desire to wake up and instill a desire to grow in maturity. The Holy Spirit will bring to light hidden issue and unhealed wounds, which will enlighten and inspire us to achieve sensible goals and continue in God's recovery program.

We are to learn to work together in love and help each other work with the Lord in His love—seeking and speaking the truth about our issues and becoming transformed on the inside. To wake up and grow into becoming Christ-like in character, and to develop our own healthy and unique personality.

"Rather, speaking the truth in love, we are to grow up in every way into him who is the head, into Christ" (Ephesians 4:15).

Journal Date: ____/____/____

Jump Start Life Now

Class Topic No. 21: Forgiveness and Accountability

Date: ____/____/____ Speaker: _____

Share with the group....
- One thing that you are grateful for today.
- One accomplishment this week that helped in your recovery.
- One insight on <u>why</u> things went wrong and how to change the <u>why</u>.
- One thing you did to help someone else.

Quote for the day:

Unforgiveness lodged within the heart turns to bitterness over time. Bitterness will form a type of mental and spiritual gangrene that, if left to itself will destroy life and liveliness. (See Luke 6:37-38.)

We must learn how to completely forgive anyone who has ever hurt us, from the heart. However, we must hold anyone accountable to stop hurting us or others when we see and realize their abuse. If the abuser does not change, we have the responsibility to protect ourselves and others. We must stop associating with them. If necessary, we should seek legal help to apply authority to stop the abuse. (See Matthew 18:15-18.)

Forgiving from the heart requires working through the emotional and mental pain of the wounds from the hurtful person and the event or situation. Forgiving and then forgetting, without working to resolve the inner turmoil and pain caused by the person that wronged us, is another form of suppressing issues of the heart. These unresolved issues become ticking time bombs.

Unforgiveness works against us and allows the devil to protect evil abusers. When we forgive completely by resolving all internal issues, this frees us up from the lingering hurt and puts the perpetrator under God's judgments and wrath.

Class Discussion and Comments:
- Why is it hard to forgive another who has wounded us?
- Just mentally forgiving another does not work. What does it feel like to forgive another from the heart?
- How do we know if we still lodge bitterness and resentment to another from past wounds and disappointments?
- Held resentments breeds a "get even" internal agenda in life and "bitter expectations" about life that indirectly effects the course of life. Unforgiveness can spew bitterness towards others later in life, where friends and loved ones suffer from our inner turmoil—we then wound others for something they never did.
- How can we hold hurtful people accountable to change? What can we do if they won't change?

Class Notes:

_____

_____

_____

The Disease of Bitter Jealousy and Selfish Ambition

"But if you have bitter jealousy and selfish ambition in your hearts, do not boast and be false to the truth. This is not the wisdom that comes down from above, but is earthly, unspiritual, demonic. For where jealousy and selfish ambition exist, there will be disorder and every vile practice" (James 3:14-16).

Have you ever endured a bitter person? Did you pick up on the attitudes that lead to strife, sarcasm, contentious or inflammatory remarks that frequently incites arguments. Did you notice how these things cause low morale and despondency?

The disease of bitter jealousy motivates unhealthy competitiveness where shortcuts, back stabbing, and greed becomes a practice of climbing to the top of life. Whether it be in work, relationships, church or fellowship, and even within family relations.

Most often, sibling rivalry is the source of bitter jealousy, where parental favoritism was practiced in the family of origin.

Many suffer from receiving less than others in childhood and even later in life as young adults. The devil uses jealousy to help embittered people create a boastful approach to living as they subtly grasp and often ruthlessly claw to have more and more.

The only cure to the disease of bitterness is the truth found in the Gospel of Christ and realizing how to be content with what we have and trust God for what we need. Having this attitude of heart brings freedom.

However, to get to that blessed freedom requires that we allow God to search out our true intentions of heart and work with Him to resolve any stale-bitter unforgiveness from our past forgotten, unhealed wounds.

Journal Date: ____/____/____

Jump Start Life Now

Class Topic No. 22: Holding Ground While Advancing

Date: ____/____/____ Speaker: _____

Share with the group....

- One thing that you are grateful for today.
- One accomplishment this week that helped in your recovery.
- One insight on <u>why</u> things went wrong and how to change the <u>why</u>.
- One thing you did to help someone else.

Quote for the day:

Therefore do not throw away your confidence, which has a great reward. For you have need of endurance, so that when you have done the will of God you may receive what is promised."
Hebrews 10:35-36

Class Discussion and Comments:

- Life will always have its share of suffering. The key is to understand that suffering is part of life and it includes everyone—you are not alone. The enemy of your life wants you to give up, for he knows if you hold on, you will receive what God has promised.
- One key in holding our ground is to continue fighting. But learn to contend for God's will and fight for what is right, trusting that God will give you strength to overcome or deliver you from anything that is too much to handle.
- When suffering in life's battles, make sure you are suffering because you are advancing in the right direction. We suffer extra for hanging on to wrong goals or clinging to the pleasures of sin.
- There are people who don't experience suffering. Don't be envious, for when we suffer, we learn how to grow in character and walk with the Lord in a stronger and deeper manner.
- We must trust God when things seem to be unmanageable and seek God's help.
- Sometimes God's help seems late and not how we would like to see it come. However, his help is never too late, and as we mature and look back, we learn he provided the right kind of help at the right time.
- Our challenge is to walk by faith and hang on to our progress. Resist self-pity and envy of others and hold the ground that you have gained, waiting for God to restore your life, advancing you to a higher level of living by faith. When we learn to properly manage what we have now, God will widen your scope of responsibility and provide more resources to meet your needs and responsibilities—that is, when are you become mature enough that you won't misuse or abuse the His temporal blessings.

Class Notes:

_____
_____
_____
_____

Up and down at first, then steady progress

Consider him who endured from sinners such hostility against himself, so that you may not grow weary or fainthearted" (Hebrews 12:3).

Overcoming wounds to the spirit and damaged emotions, along with changing self-destructive behavior and wrong choices does not happen overnight. Nor does the up and down feelings of hopeless, anxiety, and depression go away immediately.

In fact, as we start God's recovery program our ill feelings seem to be strong as ever. The key to overcoming the rough start of recovery is to understand that you have the Holy Spirit to aid and comfort you. Turning to the Lord when feeling overwhelmed will give the Holy Spirit opportunity to comfort and encourage you and bring to light why you feel so down and why you are having confusing self-defeating thoughts.

Partner with others who are honest and who also have faith in God. Share each other's burdens. If you get knocked down, don't become discouraged, but rather admit the issue and talk it out. Continue to be in fellowship with likeminded people who know what it means to fight to overcome troubling feelings, addictions, and despair.

"Brothers, if anyone is caught in any transgression, you who are spiritual should restore him in a spirit of gentleness. Keep watch on yourself, lest you too be tempted. Bear one another's burdens, and so fulfill the law of Christ" (Galatians 6:1-2).

Many in recovery go to church, yet do not receive proper encouragement and support on a regular basis. They then fall away, and give up, because it is so bumpy at first and they become convinced that they can't make it, or that they were never born again.

As you advance and continue to work with God and others who are likeminded, (who know how to support others in recovery), the bumps smooth out and steady progress becomes the norm. Life is changed because of persevering with God and by steadily working on issues—becoming changed on the inside.

As the Apostle wrote to Christians at Philippi, *"And I am sure of this, that he who began a good work in you will bring it to completion"* (Philippians 1:6).

Journal Date: ____/____/____

Jump Start Life Now

Living Within Your Means

Americans have a love affair with pleasure, fun, and material wealth where credit cards become the shortcut to having and owning. Per the latest Federal Reserve figures, we have $853 billion in credit card debt. As a nation, we love to shop, but often consumerism leads to burdening debt creating monthly financial struggles.

Wounded people most often suffer from childhood depravity or had far less in clothing, toys, and vacations then neighbors and school mates. Then as adults, bitter jealousy can seep in and drive envious longing for these things. These issues in our lives give credit card companies and lenders a natural path to ensnare wounded people into living beyond their means by using credit.

Learn to work with the Lord in healing these hidden pitfalls. The main effects of bitter jealousy spawns beliefs and feelings that "life is not fair and too short to miss out." This wrong inner mindset drives the less affluent to compete with the affluent (rich) in society. Jesus said: *"Do not lay up for yourselves treasures on earth, where moth and rust destroy and where thieves break in and steal, but lay up for yourselves treasures in heaven, where neither moth nor rust destroys and where thieves do not break in and steal. For where your treasure is, there your heart will be also"* (Matthew 6:19-21). In addition, Christ said, *"For what does it profit a man to gain the whole world and forfeit his soul?"* (Mark 8:36)

Many crave for more and more, and thus fall in love with money. *"But those who desire to be rich fall into temptation, into a snare, into many senseless and harmful desires that plunge people into ruin and destruction. For the love of money is a root of all kinds of evils. It is through this craving that some have wandered away from the faith and pierced themselves with many pangs"* (1 Timothy 6:9-10).

The Apostle Paul further explains: *"As for the rich in this present age, charge them not to be haughty, nor to set their hopes on the uncertainty of riches, but on God, who richly provides us with everything to enjoy. They are to do good, to be rich in good works, to be generous and ready to share, thus storing up treasure for themselves as a good foundation for the future, so that they may take hold of that which is truly life"* (1 Timothy 6:17-19).

Based on these passages, I developed a proper understanding about the rich that I want to share with you. The following tip can help you overcome jealousy of others.

If a rich person gained his or her affluence with hard work and are rich in helping others, then to me that is great. However, if the rich gained wealth by greed and lust, then they are in a very terrible trap—with no way out. Thus, I do want to be jealous of either, but I have learned to be content with what I have and trust God to increase my wealth as needed. (See James 5:1-11.)

Here are some more tips to make sure you never end up with more monthly needs and expenses than money.

Know your income and expenses: The first thing you need to know is what's coming in and what's going out. Make a list of all income you have from your job, side work, benefits, pension or anywhere else. Then make a list of every bill you have, from rent to car payment. (Don't forget bills that may not arrive monthly, like car insurance.)

These are your **fixed expenses** – the ones you have limited control over. The difference between your income and fixed expenses is what's left for the expenses you can control—your **variable and discretionary expenses**.

Most of us have sufficient income to cover our fixed expenses. After all, we wouldn't have taken on obligations we couldn't pay. It's the variable and discretionary expenses that so often get out of control.

Track your expenses: A spending plan, known as a budget, is the single best way to ensure you live within your means. A spending plan is exactly what the name implies: It lays out what you plan to spend. This plan will keep tabs on your progress, or lack thereof. A budget is necessary for tracking what you spend your money on. Budgeting used to be a difficult process of writing down everything you spent, dividing the expenditures into categories, adding them up, and comparing those totals with your plan.

These days online budgeting services make the process easy. Using a spreadsheet on your computer will also make it very easy to track and total the budget when new items are added or adjusting individual items. If you want to live within your means and reach your goals, you must track where your money's going. It's the only way to nip problems in the bud.

Separate wants and needs: When it comes to shopping, knowing the difference between a want and a need will help you stay out of debt. Before you make a purchase, ask yourself if you really need it. If you don't, wait before you buy it. A good way to avoid compulsive spending is to use the 48-hour rule. If you see something you want to buy but don't think you absolutely need it, wait 48 hours before buying it. Often, you will change your mind.

Don't compete: Don't fall victim to the "keeping up with the Joneses" mentality. Sure, your friends or neighbors might drive nicer cars, have the newest technology, or take expensive vacations, but that doesn't mean you should do the same.

Think of it this way: Your neighbor might have financed that Mercedes, put the new flat-screen on his credit card, and taken out a personal loan to pay for a vacation. You're not a lemming; don't follow the group off a cliff.

Pay in cash: It isn't always easy or immediately gratifying but adopting a pay-in-cash lifestyle can save you from falling into a debt trap. Wait and save for that new TV by watching on your lap top or on your old TV. You won't miss a thing while waiting. Marketing experts know what button to push to influence consumers to buy before waiting and saving. If you can't afford to buy something now, don't pull out the plastic. Instead, save up and pay cash.

Keep an emergency fund: Life is unpredictable. Emergencies spring up, and if you have an emergency fund to tap, then you won't have to take on debt. You may not be able to do this right away, however, as soon as possible start saving funds for three to six-month equal to expenses. When something goes wrong, and it will, you won't have to reach for your credit card or take out a loan to pay for it.

Save money wherever and whenever possible: Saving money will help you stop overextending yourself financially. Try these tips to get started:
- **Never walk into the grocery store unprepared or hungry.** Before you shop, clip or print out coupons, check the weekly circular, and make a list. When you go grocery shopping on an empty stomach, your stomach pushes for things you don't need.
- **Don't pay retail.** Sign up for a store's newsletters to get coupons and learn about sales. When shopping online, always compare prices at several sites and look for a coupon or promotional code. Sites like Dealnews, Savings.com and RetailMeNot will help you find the best deal.
- **Skip designer coffee.** Sure, it tastes fantastic, but it's also $4.50 a cup. Make your coffee at home.
- **Buy secondhand.** You can find incredible deals at garage sales or in thrift shops.
- **Banking options:** Many banks offer automatic savings accounts. For every transaction using your debit card, the bank automatically transfers $1.00 into your savings account. If you use a debit card attached to your checking account, make sure you enter and tract all transactions in your check register when using a debit card. Many lose track and become overdrawn on their checking account and accrue fees that mount up quickly

Jump Start Life Now

Cut down on expenses: If you're still struggling to live within your means, take a hard look at your expenses. There is probably something you can cut out or at least cut down on. For example:
- Gym memberships.
- Hair and nail salons.
- Cable TV.
- Cellphone bills.
- Shopping trips.
- Go through your bills and cancel any service you don't use frequently. For the stuff you do use, call the provider and see if you can get a better deal.

Boost your income: If all else fails, boost your income. The simplest and most gratifying way is to make more at your current job by getting a raise. If that's not in the cards and you routinely find yourself struggling to make ends meet, it might be time to look for a better-paying job. Of course, there are many other ways to increase your income, from selling your stuff to side jobs to turning a hobby into a business. Where there's a will, there's usually a way. Ask the Lord for help in prayer, and patiently wait.

Don't deprive yourself: While this is the last tip, it's the most important one. When you hear terms like "living within your means," especially when combined with words like "budget," it's natural to think about deprivation. You might think there's no difference between "budget" and "diet." They're both about deprivation, right? Wrong.

A diet *is* deprivation: Cottage cheese isn't anything close to ice cream. Living within your means, on the other hand, doesn't have to be about deprivation. Spending less on insurance by raising your deductible doesn't negatively impact your life. Nor does having dinner at home with friends instead of paying big bucks at a restaurant. In short, you can live within your means and still enjoy life.

The trick? Substituting imagination for money. Think about what you really enjoy — then find a way to get it for less.

Overcoming our Toxic Culture

We live in a culture inundated with mental and emotional pressures that often start in early childhood. Most in crisis had a troubling time growing up; poor parenting, abuse, poverty, and learning challenges. Now as recovering adults we are continually bombarded with persuasive messages and images that try to pry money out of our wallets or push us to indulge in legal but potentially addictive processes.

The placement of junk food in grocery store isles is designed to initiate compulsive buying and get children grabbing, begging, and throwing tantrums.

The pressure to have a newer and better product, even though the current product works perfectly fine is in most advertisements or TV commercial.

Our free market culture operates on mixing needs and wants together to program consumers to buy without wisdom, reason, necessity, or with thrift.

Entertainment media pushes sex, violence, infatuation and instant gratification. Genuine love and sacrifice are rarely portrayed. Greed and lust are promoted with few examples of morality, character, the sacrifices of self-discipline, abstinence and patience. Rather, instant gratification has become the selling point in getting people to spend, spend, spend, consume, consume, consume. An entitlement mentality is quashing the need for waiting, saving, study, and hard work.

Most in society, especially wounded people are aloof to these subliminal toxic messages (hidden and affecting the unconscious). These poisonous influences easily aggravate mental and emotional disorders and push people who lack self-control into craving money to buy luxuries and indulge in pain suppressing activities. Many become overtaken and fall into a dysfunctional lifestyle and often self-destructive addictions and behaviors. And most of these addictive processes are legal, but for so many these influences eventually lead to very harmful and illegal addictions, such as alcohol abuse, opiates and other illegal pain killing drugs.

Our toxic culture pushes society into craving "good times, fun times" indulgences. Those in recovery need to examine societal influences that say you deserve the best, so indulge, let go and have fun. The desire for good times drives obsessive behaviors. Few are aware of the toxic pull upon passivity of the wounded. Just one hour of viewing TV or listening to pop radio can que and drive someone's craving issues over the top.

We need to become aware of the influences that spawn inactivity, lethargy, procrastination, and envy. We must learn to fight and overcome spontaneous urges that knock the bottom out of our savings and derail good financial planning. We must become wise to hucksters who sell get-rich-quick schemes and fun times.

Part of recovery is no longer needing to keep pace with our neighbor's or our friend's affluent life style. The world of marketing takes advantage of self-pity and jealousy, so become aware of your true motives for going into debt or lusting after a new fancy car or a bigger home, designer clothes and other non-essential items—learn to buy needed items that are lesser priced but do just as well.

Another area that those in recovery need to overcome is magic thinking concerning dealing with challenging issues in life. Learn to deal with problems effectively and soon as possible, before they become a crisis. Don't stay in a childish pretend world and shrink back from making those hard choices as soon as practical, and in wisdom. Living a life that takes shortcuts and avoids hard decisions will eventually pile up and explode like a volcano.

As you learn to slow down and consider what influences and motivates you into doing things that are not helpful, meaningful, needful, or practical—it will become much easier to say no and stave off the subliminal toxic messaging that is all around us.

Towards Making a Home

You may be experiencing homelessness or living in temporary living quarters or have trouble finding a suitable home to rent. Do your best to find temporary stable housing for you (and your family) to become stable and then seek help to obtain a more permanent housing and hopefully direct you towards making a home for yourself (and your family).

The keys in making a new home or restoring proper living conditions are as follows:

1) **Ask for help.**
2) **Practice patient and persistence.**
3) **Don't give up hope when you meet delays, keep advancing and planning.**
4) **Ask in prayer, your Heavenly Father knows you need a home.**

And one more thing: Keep motivated, there is a special freedom when we become self-sufficient and independent by living in our own home and making a way for ourselves.

Housing: On page 9 we list resources for immediate housing assistance, seniors and disabled housing assistance, and transitional housing. Become familiar with these resources and don't hesitate in pursing help from people on the contact list in this section.

Help from Friends and Family: Often a friend or extended family member may offer temporary living quarters and financial help. Be careful not to strain any relationship by imposing upon those who will have a hard time providing help. This type of quick fix answer to your problem can create a worse situation.

Often it is an extended family member or a close friend's help in your past that partially enabled wrong choices that led to your current situation, so be careful.

Patience and Hope: It is easy to become discouraged. Restoring housing and making a new home does not happen instantly. Share concerns with those helping and listen to sound advice and encouragement.

Cover Letter and Resume

"Any other people skills, besides 400 Facebook friends?"

The First Contact – the Cover Letter

How do you get noticed to get an interview—to rise above the competition and land the job?

It all starts with the cover letter because it is generally the first document a hiring professional will read. Make your cover letter stand out above the rest by following the seven interview-getting, attention-grabbing cover letter tips.

1: Just three paragraphs on one page: introduction, skills/qualifications, and ASK for the interview in the last paragraph.

2: Keep each paragraph to just three or four punchy, well-written sentences. Make it "easy on the eyes."

3: Allow your text to breathe by including plenty of white space. This means big margins, and double spacing between paragraphs, and one and a half spaces between lines.

4: Create bullets and numbered lists to help readers scan quickly.

5: Use bolding occasionally to emphasize important points, and to increase readability. (Don't use too much—just a few important lines throughout to break things up a little.)

6: Proofread your cover letter and correct spelling, grammar, and punctuation. This is an obvious one, but if it's not handled, it can ruin any chance you have of landing the interview.

7: Double check your contact information, and don't forget to hand sign the letter. Nothing is more embarrassing (and deal-breaking) than getting your own phone number or address wrong.

Your Cover Letter Writing Process: First, write a cover letter that gives an introduction and states your intent for applying. It must also discuss your qualifications quickly, simply, and concisely. Finally, it must ask for the interview. Next, go through the seven tips above to make sure they are all covered before sending off the cover letter with your resume.

If you follow all this advice, the hiring manager will have no choice but to give you a call, assuming you have presented the right skills for the job in a compelling way. It'll be obvious that you are trustworthy and dependable, and that you are definitely someone to contact for the position.

Most job seekers do NOT pay enough attention to the cover letter, and simply "throw one together" as an afterthought. You have an opportunity to rise above the fold with your cover letter—enough to single you out for the job interview.

The Resume that Closes the Interview

We all want a chance to interview and show what we are made of. But first, make a good impression. Here are some Resume tips to help you get that interview!

Keep it direct: You don't have to make your resume extremely detailed. Think of it as a tool for getting your foot in the door, you will have time to elaborate when you have your interview.

Don't worry about including your objective, the employer should be able to figure out what your objective is based on your resume. Also, don't put reference information on your resume. This will just take up valuable space. Most of the time, if needed, employers will likely request you to include your references on the job application you fill out for them.

Jump Start Life Now

Sell Yourself: View your resume as a commercial. You only have a few moments to capture your audience's attention. Don't be afraid to show your strengths via positive keywords, you're selling yourself!! Don't be modest. When putting your resume together, keep this tip in mind. Review the job description and then review your resume. You should try to make the two connect and emphasize the information (ex. Qualifications, experience and skills) that the employer is seeking. This will help your resume stand out.

Layout should show the following:
- Contact Information
- Education (list your GPA, leaving it out will leads the employer to assume it's not the best)
- Relevant Experience/Work History
- Skills (Quickbooks, Excel Knowledge, etc.)
- Honors/Achievements

Make it Neat: The layout of the resume is important, it should be easy to look at and remain consistent throughout the document. There's a good chance if you don't like the way it looks, neither will the recruiter. Keep all your information on one page, unless you're a CEO with 25+ years of experience (yes, I might be slightly exaggerating) you don't need more than one page for your resume. And don't make your font smaller than size 11 or use less than the standard one-inch margins just to keep it one page.

Content: Easy on the contact information, you don't need to put more than one address and phone number. Putting your cell phone number is best and provide your email address. Provide specific details about your work experience (specific skills that you have acquired and how it was utilized on the job). Mention any foreign language you speak or understand.

Don't use colors, please don't. You can show your personality during the interview, not through a piece of paper. Proofread, proofread and proofread again!!

Job Interviews and Personal Presentation

1. Never, ever arrive late.
2. Do not speak negatively about current or past employers.
3. Never dress casually or in evening cloths.
4. Arrive neatly groomed. Don't look disheveled, like you just got out of bed.
5. Never chew gum.
6. Fill out employer application completely unless told differently. "See Resume" is not appreciated.
7. Never move interview chair unless invited to do so.
8. Avoid slang, i.e., ain't, yeh, huh, etc.
9. Be polite and friendly to everyone you meet including the receptionist.
10. Always take several resume originals with you.

Since we recommend not including references with the resume, have them (typed) with you. Make sure you note relationship, how long and from where, plus contact phone number.

Work Skills Development

Communication Skills: This doesn't mean you must become a brilliant orator or writer. It does mean you should learn to express yourself well, whether it's writing a coherent memo, persuading others with a presentation or just being able to calmly explain to a team member what you need.

Teamwork and Collaboration: Employers want employees who play well with others—who can effectively work as part of a team. Sometimes you will need be a leader—sometimes be a good follower. You may have to monitor the progress of a project or meet deadlines and work with others across the organization to achieve a common goal.

Adaptability: As you get settle in doing your job, resist the mindset of stagnation, where you develop a reputation of being set in your ways. Growing and succeeding in most organizations requires a passion for learning and the ability to stretch your skills to adapt to the changing needs of the organization.

Problem Solving: Be prepared for the "how did you solve a problem?" interview question with several examples. Have in mind specific examples where you solved a tough business problem or participated in the solution. Be prepared to explain what you did, how you approached the problem, how you involved others and what the outcome was—in real, measurable results.

Critical Observation: Collecting data and manipulate it is needful, however you must also be able to analyze and interpret it. What story does the data tell? What questions are raised? Are there different ways to interpret the data? Learn to give a business summary and highlight the key areas for attention and suggest possible next steps. Become a critical thinker on the job, observing problem areas and considering recommendations for more smooth, efficient, cost effective ways to improve operations.

Conflict Resolution: The ability to persuade, negotiate and resolve conflicts is crucial if you plan to move up. Learn to improve your skill in developing mutually beneficial relationships in the organization. Learn to influence, persuade, and negotiate with people towards win-win solutions that serves the best interests of the company and the individuals involved.

Soft Skill Sets—Show them don't tell: How do you prove you're proficient at, say, critical observation? Demonstrating these soft skills can be more difficult than just listing concrete accomplishments like listing sales achievements or how many finished products were produced under your supervision. We must learn to persuade hiring managers that we have what they need. To demonstrate the skill to communicate, start with the obvious by making sure there are no typos in your resume or cover letter. Enhance your communication ability by writing an achievement statement on your resume or cover letter. Instead of stating, you have great oral and written communication skills by giving some examples: *presented workshops that effectively increased sales, wrote new procedures for procurement that effectively reduced department operations costs.*

Learn and Improve Soft Skills: The good news is that, like any skill, soft skills can be learned. The better news? Boosting your soft skills not only gives you a leg up on a new job or a promotion, but these skills also have obvious applications in all areas of a person's life, both professional and personal. You can improve these skills by taking college course that mix technology with effective written and verbal communications. Or enroll in writing or public speaking courses and leadership skill classes. Hook up with a mentor to target specific skills, or volunteer for a nonprofit to help build soft skills.

Jump Start Job Search

Many in crisis, who need a job do not have transportation. (Refer to the resource page for transportation services.) Don't let lack of personal transportation hold you back. Rides can be arranged and often positions are available within walking distance from where you are staying or your home or the shelter.

So, what can you do now—especially if you are currently out of work and in a crisis—in finding a job? The following 10 things may help you become employed now, and give your job search a jump start. Becoming employed, even if it is a low entry job, will help bring back confidence and add to your stabilization.

1. Colorado Workforce Center and Temporary Job Agencies: Utilize the Colorado Workforce Center 719-275-7408, located at 3224-B Independence Rd. Canon City. The center offers numerous resources to improve your hire-ability and will help you land a job. Another way to find income, even while looking for permanent position is to take a temp position. Temporary agencies are out there to help all kinds of workers, and depending on your situation, you may find more than one that hires out people with your skills.

2. Identify at Least Five Prospective Employers: Conduct a search (Workforce Center, via the phone book, Chamber of Commerce, Google, etc.) for prospective employers who hire job-seekers with your skills. Conduct research on each employer you find that fits your criteria so that you can use that information to enhance your cover letter, resume, and application. Once you have the information you need, apply directly to the hiring manager (for your position) of each employer. Cold calls can be helpful, so don't be afraid to make phone calls and knock on doors.

3. Find and apply to at least one real job opening: Using all the tools available to you — local job ads, industry-specific job boards, and general job boards — locate and apply to at least one job opening. Do not, however, spend the bulk of your day on job boards because some of the "open" job openings may be no longer be available (or perhaps never were). Still, take the time to conduct a search as you may be able to find hidden gems that you could not find through other job-search methods. Finally, remember that networking and direct contact yield much greater success than applying to jobs online.

Even if you feel you have done this step already, make it a point today to contact people in your network about any new job leads. Ask the closest people to you to contact their family and friends to truly utilize the power of this tool. Remember that you are simply asking about any information about potential job openings and other contacts to talk to; you are not asking people for a job. The more networking you do, the more likely your success in finding a new job.

5. Schedule a meeting with a career expert: If you're having a hard time finding a new job, you may have a problem with your job-hunting tactics that you will never be able to identify without the assistance of a career expert. Again, make appointment with the Colorado Workforce office or seek help from others who can help mentor and give pointers.

6. Find additional people to add to your career network: Because networking is the most powerful job-search tool available to job-seekers, the more people you can add to your network of contacts, the more job leads you'll uncover. The most powerful network contacts are personal ones, so start here by finding and attending a networking event, volunteering in your community, joining a professional or industry organization, and asking for introductions to people from your family and friends

7. Revise, revamp, and improve your resume: Your resume is your most important job-search tool, and based on experiences, just about every job-seeker has room for improvement in crafting a resume that will help you obtain job interviews. Refer to cover letter and resume section.

8. Sharpen your interviewing skills: The job interview is your chance to shine—to sell your unique mix of experience, education/training, and skills to the hiring manager(s). If you are going on first interviews, but never getting invited back, your interviewing style may be flawed. Two of the most common flaws for job-seekers is failing to anticipate potential interview questions and not developing strategic responses to those questions. If you're struggling with interviewing, you can try practicing mock interviews with friends, family, or career experts. You can also try asking for feedback from hiring managers who did not hire you.

9. Research and request informational interviews: One of the most underutilized tools of job-hunting is the informational interview. This tool is most useful when you are changing careers and trying to break into a new career field, but it is a technique all job-seeker can use. An informational interview is a request in which you seek to learn useful facts about a career, industry, or company. Remember that these are NOT job interviews, and job-seekers should not try to turn them into one. Instead, use these to learn more and build your network.

10. Follow-up all pending job applications: Take the time today to contact all the employers with whom you have applied or had interviews. Most employers view follow-up as showing interest and a desire for the job, so do not be afraid to not only follow up today, but again next week and the week after (unless the employer tells you not to bother). Just remember to be professional and polite when contacting the employers. You can follow up by phone or email.

Finally, stay as positive as you can with your job-search. Employers and hiring managers can sense desperation, fear, frustration, and anger—these are typical out-of-work job-seeker emotions—so always try and enter each situation with a positive outlook and confidence that this time you will succeed. And importantly, pray and ask God for wisdom, a calm heart, and direction.

Skills and Principles that Help Manage Living While in Crisis

Restoring Dreams

Bucked off life's horse? Dust yourself off, get back on and learn what NOT to do.

Working through difficult situations, especially the loss of your home, or fighting for custody of your children, recovering from domestic violence, or reeling from the devastation of divorce is emotionally draining and mentally discouraging.

Hope and faith in tomorrow can fly out the window and depression and panic can take over your whole temperament.

If direction and hope are not restored, these kind of devastating events and situations can lead to even deeper tragedy through uncontrolled behavior easily driven by bitterness, rage, revenge, and hate.

You may have lost your home through bad choices, wrong behavior, a destructive life style or the results of a destructive relationship. Whatever the situation, you need to evaluate what happened, why it happened and work towards changing yourself on the inside.

A major trap for victims of a destructive relationship is the desire to change your partner or find a new partner that is agreeable to your set ways and inner expectations of a perfect partner. You may be the victim again and again, because of your unwillingness to see your own unhealthy issues that helped incite and perpetuate friction in past relationships.

Finding a new relationship or moving to a new region is like "turning over a new leaf" (an idiom that means starting over or reforming oneself). Many start over this way and fall right back into the same dysfunctional lifestyle or fall unconsciously into another destructive relationship. Changing our own inner issues of heart and building proper character will allow real change that is lasting, healthy, and will lead to a functional and fulfilling life.

We can't change others, we can only change ourselves and learn to hold others accountable to change without controlling, manipulating, or being caustic and demanding. Many in troubled situations can learn to make inner character change, often by learning to create a stronger and more ethical personality.

However, deep inner change can only come from the help of Christ, if we learn to work with him, in cooperation and understanding. To work with Christ's power to achieve inner character change, we must allow him to remove our blinders, to see the truth about ourselves, and let Christ (knowledge of Him) be our model to be transformed into: *"And we all, with unveiled face, beholding the glory of the Lord, are being transformed into the same image from one degree of glory to another. For this comes from the Lord who is the Spirit"* (2 Corinthians 3:18).

Often victims need to stay the victim because that is how they identify being loved. Women tend to hook up with a man that was like their father's short falls, and mate with the same type of character or the opposite: hook up with their fantasized dream mate opposite of an absentee or abusive dad.

Likewise, most men fall into the same fate. Until these almost invisible internal tendencies are healed and changed, trying to restore your dreams for life and live again will be subjected again and again to self-sabotaging troubles.

You must work on changing internally (we recommend God's help) before trying to get your dreams restored. One of the worse things to do is to attempt to restore you lost dreams and life's promises before you have learned your lessons. Although, some can start to put dreams bad together and, in the process, make appropriate internal changes. And most people in crisis, are in crisis by making bad choices along the way that seemed to be good at the time, then after picking themselves up to start over, only to repeat the same mistakes in a similar, yet in a veiled manner.

Furthering Your Education

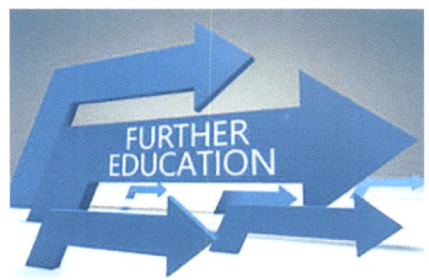

Most wounded people learn to just survive with a adequate job and make a marnginal living. Many in childhood had their desire to learn become crushed. Wounded people must fight to restore the desire to gain knowledge and learn wisdom to apply knowledge correctly.

Continueing to learn must become a steady desire that is managed in a healthy manner. *"The heart of him who has understanding seeks knowledge, but the mouths of fools feed on folly."* (Proverbs 15:14).

A college education is good for some people, however, knowledge gained in everyday living and work is often found to be more important than a person who has amassed degrees, yet lacks understanding through experiencial knowledge, knowhow, and wisdom.

Many universitie give credit recognition for work and life experience. I have found that additional formal education beyond high school was good for me. However, because I had years of experience in the military, construction and manaul labor work, and even work that I did in my youth, gave me a practical knowledge base for living, interacting with people, communicating and working effectively.

Two things that everyone should continue to improve upon are, communicating effectively and listening appropriately. 1) Always strive to improve your understanding of proper use of words, both in writing and speaking. 2) Learn to be attentive, by tuning out meaningless background noise, and tune your listening abilities to seek truth.

Furthing your education to expand your knowledge and wisdon on how to speak from the heart truthfully and wisely, and learning how to filter out rhetoric and hyperbole (exageration) that manipulates and decieves—will help further your education daily.

As far as furthering your education formerly, choose a field of interest. Discover what you like to do in work or as a profession. Then plan financially and plan your schedule in choosing an appropriate higher learning opportunity: GED, vocational school, community college, university, and do not rule out on the job training and industry specific classes provided by your employer.

When you start the work of higher education be prepared to make sacrifices of the unimportant time consuming things in life. When you hit bumps in the road and feel like quitting, don't quit. Muster up the courage and determination to continue on until your studies are completed.

College can be a challenge, and you do not have to live on the campus to receive a college degree. You can attend in spurts, by going to night classes, or attend online. Many accredited universitities have excellent distant learning programs. Be leary of the scam vocational and speciality schools. Check out their licensing and accreditations.

You may suffer from a learning disability. Most people with learning disabilities can overcome the disability through special programs. Many learning challenges stem from past trauma and inappropriate pressure during gradeschool. Check out tutoring and other learning programs to help.

I had a math phobia that began in the fourth grade. My father tried to help me memorize the times table by making me stand at attention during recital, and then hit me when I made a mistake. He used boxing gloves so as to not really hurt me, never-the-less, all through highschool I hated math and english and cheated my way through algebra, geometry and trigonometry.

Later in the Marine Corps, while attending basic electronics school, my math phobia almost caused me to fail in the first week. Back then slide rules, not calculators were used in calculating basic formulas to determine such things as voltage, resistance and current values. These challenges aroused my my mental block.

If it were not for a patient Marine Corps instructor tutoring me, I would have failed and then become a radio operator and likely shipped to Viet Nam. A higher fear of dying on patrol packing a radio helped me study and overcome. In the end, I went over two years going to electronic schools in the Corps, was an honor graduate, and then reieved training to be an instructor teaching field telephone switchboard repair.

Not all who struggle with a mental block or a learning disability can overcome in the same way. Years later, as I struggled in life from past unresolved issues and with sound counsel and help by the Holy Spirit, I was able to achieve deeper changes concerning my latent fears and insecurities that hampered learning and my ability to comprehend.

Jump Start Life Now

Parenting & Significant Relationships

Raising children properly should take precedence over any parental selfish interests and past times interests that make for absentee parents. This includes single parents, even though raising children in this situation is much harder.

Planning personal timeouts must include proper care for children by responsible and mature people. Leaving children unattended who are not of the age to care for themselves, even for short time is unacceptable and unlawful.

Most adults who struggle in life have the primary cause traced back to a dysfunctional or abusive family of origin. The key is to break the generational cycle and not hand down to your own children a variation of the dysfunction or abuse. It is important to learn to deal with your own issues and not let them affect your children.

Parents who struggle with internal issues one way or another, inflict upon their children wounds that will tend to be passed on in similar forms of dysfunction and internal struggles. Resentment towards the responsibilities in parenting mount up and effect children. Left to grind on in frustration often ignites anger expressed toward children. Unfortunately, in many cases resentment turns to abuse.

Parental anger often turns to yelling, cursing, threatening, and abusive discipline toward children, often these issues can lead to evil vindictive parental abuse. Just expressing angry hateful words can do great damage.

James, the brother of Jesus and author of the epistle of James in the New Testament addresses what wrong words can do: *"And the tongue is a fire, a world of unrighteousness. The tongue is set among our members, staining the whole body, setting on fire the entire course of life, and set on fire by hell. For every kind of beast and bird, of reptile and sea creature, can be tamed and has been tamed by mankind, but no human being can tame the tongue. It is a restless evil, full of deadly poison"* (James 3:6-8).

Parents can reverse these staining affects from past improper parenting by becoming healed themselves and begin to express genuine love towards each child in their care, without favoritism.

The following are four major principles to remember:

1) Do not put false responsibility upon a child to make a parent feel happy. This creates an internal double-bind within the child's psyche and spirit—they will attempt to make an unhappy parent be happy and try to perform perfectly to be loved.

2) Do not provoke a child to anger through frustration, rather help a child understand and learn in a pleasant manner. If discipline is necessary, it must be carried with love, respect, and with demonstrated understanding for the child.

3) All discipline should be carried out in love (not harshly), fairly, consistently, in firmness, and with the expression of forgiveness. Parents need to forgive immediately, not letting the slightest disapproval show. Many parents discipline by frowning and berating for hours and even days over the smallest offense. One of the worst things parents can do is to be lazy and not properly discipline. *"Whoever spares the rod hates his son, but he who loves him is diligent to discipline him"* (Proverbs 13:24).

4) Don't be an absentee parent. Be there when they need you, support them by attending. Make promises that you can keep and try your best to keep the promises you make. Admit to them when you make a mistake, asking for thier forgiveness.

5) Live as healthy loving examples, and do not fall into the trap of parental dictatorship, commanding a "do as I say, not as I do" hypocrisy.

In doing these five principles you will train your children to live free of internal hang-ups and walk in the light of proper living: *"Train up a child in the way he should go; even when he is old he will not depart from it"* (Proverbs 22:6).

There is help in learning how to become a caring parent, making sure your children are headed in the right direction in life. Check out Family Resource Center of Fremont County 719-269-2047 or online at: www.fremontfamilyresources.org

Significant Relationships

Few people exam their real reasons for wanting a significant relationship. Most who were raised in a dysfunctional or abusive home lack internal boundaries and are not content with their own self—nor do they know who they are within.

Extreme lack of self-awareness, along with suppressed inner self-hatred camouflages internal longings to feel needed and wanted. This is a common invisible motive that leads people into wrong significant relationships.

Intimate relationships based on the need to remove internal loneliness (often associated with self-hatred) ultimately dissolves in separation or divorce, and usually becomes destructive before the relationship disintegrates. Children created in these relationships take the brunt of the damage, and almost always grow to repeat the whole relationship nightmare in their adult life.

When a person makes another responsible for their internal happiness and contentment, and to gain self-worth and self-respect—we make that person an idol or a god. This gives the other person power over the other and vice-versa, no two people should never give that kind of power to each other.

We live in a toxic culture that over emphasizes sexual and emotional intimacy. Like a powerful drug, these cultural messages and images program people to foolishly stumble to the marriage altar in bliss, only to find a short time later that it was all a lie.

Becoming healed of inner loneliness, the disliking of one's self, and correcting improper expectations of a significant relationship are the vital goals before ever considering partnering in life with another. And within that same vein, making sure the future significant other is working towards the same goal.

"Co-dependency is a possibility."

Most people have heard by now of the term dependent and co-dependent relationships. Couples caught up in this relationship sickness do not know where each other ends or begins.

Their internal selves are intermingled with each other, causing lack of individual functionality and wholeness. This sabotages positive relationship growth, and when children are thrown into this strange relationship mix, the whole family system becomes dysfunctional.

Learn how to become your own person apart from anyone else, before starting out again. Stop looking for the next trophy husband of trophy wife and begin to find and properly love yourself. When you succeed in this, you should have no problems hooking up with a significant other that lives with the same internal desire to become whole.

Already in relationship? Work with your significant other from now on, becoming your own selves apart from each other. Our advice: turn to God and the Gospel of his Son Jesus Christ. This will help you become who you were meant to be. God can restore wholeness and allow you to know and love yourself properly. By knowing and loving God above all else, he will bring you to a proper love for yourself and others. In doing this, you will never allow another person to become your god or an idol. You will be free to become a functioning human being full of life and meaning.

By following Christ, he can heal and untwist our wounded personal spirits that are intertwined. This spiritual unraveling is key to success in marriage, where two become one team. Becoming true partners in life and able to raise healthy functional children.

Jump Start Life Now

Extended Family Relationships

As adults, as stated, we need to become our own person. Not at all meaning to become controlling, repressive, a smarty pants, obnoxious, dominating or demanding. Rather to become an independent person, free from encumbrances, full of life with a heart, mind and spirit working properly.

Extended family relations can latch onto individual members, making it almost impossible to be that free and independent adult most people want to be.

What is difficult about extended family's control and its power to meddle, is its almost invisible influence. Usually it is one or two matriarchal or patriarchal individuals who rules the roost.

The controlling influence may come from a grandmother who pries into the lives of extended family members, peddling her views and opinions upon her adult children. Often casting approval upon one while subtly spewing shadowy disapproval towards another.

It may be a grandfather who creates dissention and competition between extended family units, picking favorites in doling out gifts, or pitting a son-in-law against one another son-in-law by subtlety bragging on the accomplishments of his favorite. Possibly, a daughter who pits her husband's self-worth up against her imaginary faultless father or super-hero grandfather.

Extended family should be supportive and helpful, but many extended family systems suffer the stench of gossip, dissension, competition, and sometimes outright castigation towards the so-called black sheep family member and in-laws.

Adult single people and couples who were children of a toxic family system should carefully manage involvement within their extended family system. Each should take note of the counter-productive influences and subtle negative effects of their extended family members. Couples must ensure that their own individual identity and family unit is protected and spared the often destructiveness of the toxic extended family systems.

Many try to work their way out of addictions and harmful or dysfunctional life styles only to be unconsciously pushed back down to play out their family of origin roles. Note the following:

- **Scapegoat:** The problem child in the family system becomes labeled as such and subtly influenced to continue that family expectation. Rule breaker, hostile, full of inner pain and jealousy.
- **Victim:** Alcohol or chemically dependent living in hostility, blaming others, loaded with self-pity, yet charming but covering up shame, guilt, pain, hurt and fear.
- **Family Hero:** The family caretaker who must keep those they help stay messed up and dependent. Over achiever, follows rules and seeks approval.
- **Lost Child:** Forgotten, ignored, and pushed aside, full of hurt, rejection, anxiety and hopelessness.
- **Chief Enabler:** Closest to the victim member, protects family and yet is self-righteous, and sarcastic.
- **Mascot:** Family clown, uses humor to stabilize the family and reduce stress. Uses humor to cover up internal pain.

It becomes helpful to understand where you fit within your extended family system and how your life plays out the role that you were groomed to play in maintaining family system status quo. Usually all the players revolve around one or two head rulers, either a dominating mother figure who exerts subtle influences, or a more direct in-charge head father figure leading and driving the family to carry out his idea of success. Breaking your role is a key step in your recovery, this will begin to allow yourself to become the person God originally made you to be—not the role your extended family stamps upon you.

Your Circle of Friends

"With friends like these who needs enemies."
An expression indicating that one's close associates prove more adversarial than one's opponents.

What type of friends we choose can make or break our good intentions of living life successfully. In growing up, it seemed I always chose friends who invariably helped lead me into mischief that often led to serious trouble. I had a bitter heart due to bad parenting, physical and sexual abuse, and by my family constantly moving (I attended 18 schools before graduating from high school) and several deep wounds to my spirit that produced an incorrigible and rebellious streak in my nature.

This propensity carried over into my adult life, leading me to continue to choose wrong friends that also had a bad streak within them. The seemingly good people in my life bored me or they seemed to be phony and I avoided them.

Then, trying to change my ways I hooked up with people who seemed to be very functional and religious, only to find out years later what the Apostle Paul meant when he warned that the truly evil often are disguised as good and righteous. *"For even Satan disguises himself as an angel of light. So it is no surprise if his servants, also, disguise themselves as servants of righteousness"* (2 Corinthians 11:14-15).

Even the seemingly good people can enable wounded and troubled people to stumble and fall back into sinning. It is of vital importance that we learn to choose the right circle of friends, people who want the best for us.

Today's culture is laced with a toxic "party hardy" influence and many live for today's fun in the sun and instant gratification. As you work through your recovery you will notice how certain old friends will try to enable you to wonder back into the old mind-set of letting go to have fun carelessly.

The Apostle Paul instructed the Christians at Corinth to take care who they became friends with, because many of their associates were of the philosophy that living life in the now, for its pleasures is all that counts. Paul boiled down this self-destructive mind-set as: *"Let us eat and drink, for tomorrow we die."*

The Apostle Paul clarified this idiom by stating: *"Do not be deceived: Bad company ruins good morals. Wake up from your drunken stupor, as is right, and do not go on sinning. For some have no knowledge of God"* (1 Corinthians 15:32-34).

When we seriously turn to the Lord for help in getting our lives straightened out, certain friends will recoil at the idea and out right hinder your desire and efforts in seeking to live the right way. You must be prepared for put downs and loss of friends who desire everything to stay as is.

The other aspect is making new friends that are on the same wave-length, who desire change for the good and attempt to better themselves. Even extended family and their friends can become cynical and undermine your new desire to change and try to douse your hopes for a new direction in life.

A few of our lessons and devotionals discus how to identify the wrong kind of company and learn how to avoid them or break off the relationship. Often the real dangerous so-called friends seem to be okay, at least in the beginning, however, as you mature and grow in understanding and insight concerning relationship dynamics—you will learn to politely back off and disconnect.

Unfortunately, some friends who are bad company will continue to cling and require a tough love approach in frankness and firmness. You must become willing to say no and hold your ground.

Learn to cultivate good friends who desire to live sensibly and humbly, who do not put others down, nor gossip or meddle—match up with those who encourage others and maintain a positive outlook—become friends with people who exemplify good character and courage in life challenges. Develop close friends who will tell you what you need to hear (sound counsel) yet do not condemn or insinuate that you should have done better. Friends having these qualities will help you stay the course.

Continued Recovery and Support

Getting back on your feet is your first and your foremost goal. The key afterward is staying on top of life challenges and making sure the bottom does not fall again.

Wanting the old "good-life" back again is a trap. It was that kind of lifestyle that did not work in the first place.

We have discussed the importance of maintaining proper boundaries and avoiding extended family members who enable or undermine good intentions and efforts to change. We looked at having a healthy circle of friends and dumping the game player who incites or distracts.

Now let's review some pointers on developing an ongoing support network to help your recovery take hold and continue to transform your whole life.

Part of our initial problem was lack of proper mentoring growing up. Most troubled adults lacked the nurturing and guidance that prepares people for life's challenges. This lack, coupled with a dysfunctional and/or an abusive family of origin is like having two strikes against them as they swing into adulthood.

Now, as recovering adults the missing guidance must be restored. Sure, people in crisis and struggle have wrong coping mechanisms (alcohol, drugs, sex, party lifestyle) some have street-smarts, and some take strong pride in their everyday savvy to survive. However, don't let pride stand in the way of networking with people who are functioning adults who live exemplary lives, who offer guidance and mentoring.

You may have a court order to attend a recovery support group, such as AA or another sanctioned recovery program. What we have found to be most important is having support beyond weekly meetings. Seek, find and hookup with people who have been through recovery, who demonstrate success in managing life's challenges.[2] Be leery of those who build up their own ego and find self-worth in helping others. People that have a need to show-off while helping the wounded or those in need, often do more damage than good. Jesus continually confronted the religious leader of his day because of their hypocrisy and their pride in showing off to others by doing good deeds.

If you follow Christ, seek a fellowship that addresses the issues of overcoming a wounded spirit and damaged emotions. Many churches fall into a trap of ministering primarily to those who are already well. Most offer services in religious fellowship and theological study but do not provide a solid network of mentors, counselors, and community resources that assist those in dire straits, or provide ministry for recovering addicts, or for those who suffer from post trauma distresses and disorders.

The Gospel of Christ, his teachings and the writing of the Apostles concentrate on the process of growing up into salvation (true recovery) and completing God's redemptive process that leads to wholeness. Christ's life was given as an example of what we can become when embracing God's recovery work.

---

[2] **Dry Alcoholic:** Those who are enrolled in required recovery programs often develop significant relationship or close friends from the same group. Many may stay dry and avoid relapse, however, they shift into an anti-social pattern and struggle on in life dry but dysfunctional. They develop recovery codependence with others, never changing the inner issues that drove the addiction in the beginning. The recovery group becomes a new significant relationship and becomes the new addiction.

Fellowship and Spiritual Growth

As mentioned in the continued recovery and support page (page 75), healthy fellowship or a solid network of mentors that care is vital for your continued recovery and growth.

Don't hurry through your required group meetings thinking that was part of your punishment. Rather, glean, learn, apply, and hook up with good people and find a solid fellowship (if you have become a believer in Christ by now).

Question? Are you taking notes and holding yourself accountable? Are you developing habits of slowing things down and paying attention to God given indicators and signals—are you doing the work?

Here are some more questions to ask yourself:
- Are you capturing those unwanted thoughts before you act on them?
- Are you taking notes on the emotions that override your peace and joy?
- Are you paying attention and journalizing your mood swings and compulsive behaviors?
- Are asking help from others who are part of your support network when you feel you're going to lose it or fall off the wagon.
- Are you learning to be consistent in reading the word of God and studying the context and cultural background for each passage for proper understanding? Do you ask the Holy Spirit for understanding, incite, and seek practical application in letting God's word change you?
- Are you learning to thoroughly work out the insight that God has already given you before you ask for more insight? Many plunge to the next revelation before digesting the current insight.
- Are you tracking to the root of bitter feelings of jealousy, fear and insecurity? Are you asking God to heal the associated trauma or cleanse the embedded defilements?
- Are you journalizing painful memories when they emerge—at least as soon as possible?
- Are you journalizing dreams and contemplating on what they mean and asking God for the interpretation? (However, don't become obsessed and paranoid with dreams. But rather concentrate on learning and discerning Christ's voice confirmed by God's written word and other ways that the Lord confirms his guidance and gentle voice. And be careful in sharing with others who are not likeminded but be willing to confide with those who give sound counsel and mentor.)
- Are you applying these practical devotionals in this workbook and telling God how you really feel?
- Are you avoiding short cut teachings that mask and bury issues?
- Are you learning to avoid bad company, the hyper-spiritualist believer or the religious self-righteous?
- Are you looking for and hooking up with likeminded believers who mean business with Christ, who want to change on the inside—God's way.

If you are consistently doing the above, you are demonstrating that you are headed in the right direction. The devotional-journal work is designed to help you develop habits of slowing down in life and learning how to reflect on what your thoughts and emotions are telling you, in the context of God's principles for recovery found in the Scriptures.

You cannot speed the process up, but you can slow it down by not doing the work consistently or being half-hearted. Therefore, we must in obedient in good faith—<u>trust God</u> and <u>do the work</u>.

To help with the Biblical principles of recovering from a wounded spirit and damaged emotions:

- Crushed in Spirit 2nd Edition, by Pastor Charles Pretlow ISBN 978-1-943412-16-7

To help with a solid daily devotional, we recommend the following:

- My Utmost for His Highest *by Oswald Chambers* (Classic Version)

Jump Start Life Now

About this Ministry and the Author

Pastor Charles Pretlow came to know Christ in 1973, while in the Marines Corps and then in 1974 started his ministerial work. In June 1988, he began to counsel struggling Christians. As the counseling pastor in a 400-member Foursquare fellowship, within six months of ministry, his calendar was booked three months in advance.

These troubled Christians were seeking help for a variety of issues and by word of mouth many learned about the pastor Pretlow's Holy Spirit led counseling. Most who came suffered from being reared in a dysfunctional family system; however, some cases involved severe abuse, parental abandonment, and childhood systematic sexual abuse. These cases he termed as victims of Cult Family Systems. He also has worked with victims of Satanic Ritualistic Abuse (SRA Victims).

Early on in his counseling ministry, the number of wounded Christians coming for help was nearly overwhelming. He realized that proper understanding of Scripture and being led by the Holy Spirit in facilitating God's healing power and grace was the only way to succeed. In his study of Scripture and dependence on the Holy Spirit, he soon discovered that employing the true gifts of the Holy Spirit in counseling and teaching those in his care how to work with the Holy Spirit as the ultimate counselor was the best way to help so many hurting Christians.

Through the subsequent years, pastor Pretlow found that by embracing all that Christ taught and building disciples through mentoring and counseling proved to be effective in helping struggling Christian become stable servants of Christ—having their lives restored from addictions, destructive relationships, and cycles of depression and hopelessness.

Pastor Charles Pretlow has over thirty-nine years of experience in ministry, pastoral counseling, leadership training, and ministerial recovery work. He completed his basic Bible classes at Seattle Pacific College and finished his undergraduate work at Central Washington University in Business Administration and Computer Science. This, along with his military training in leadership, as a military instructor, as well as years of coaching athletics adds to a well-rounded approach in leadership instruction, counseling, training, and mentoring those in recovery.

Our Fellowship location: MC Chapel Fellowship
Mailing Address: PO Box 857 ~ Canon City, CO 81215
Physical Location: The Abbey/St. Josephs' Building Suite 102
2951 E. Hwy 50
Canon City, CO 81212

Email: **contact@mcgmin.com**
Website: **www.mcgm.com**
Telephone: **(833) 695-1236**

Ministerial Disclaimer
The Healing and Transforming Power of Christ

We believe Christ can heal wounds to the spirit and the emotional and mental symptoms associated with a crushed spirit. This guidebook covers Biblical principles that—when understood and properly applied—will facilitate the beginning of God's healing of a wounded spirit, as well as resolve and heal damaged emotions, heal mental anguish, and change one's inner character. These principles are a direct aid for struggling believers in Christ who want to be transformed within the inner being to become Christlike in nature and attitude.

MC Global Ministries, MC Chapel Fellowship, Wilderness Voice Publishing and author, Pastor Charles Pretlow, do not claim to be a mental health organization or a mental health professional. This material contains Biblical principles and teachings that God has given to help facilitate healing for those who suffer from a wounded or crushed spirit, a broken heart, damaged emotions, and dividedness of soul and spirit.

Implementation of these principles is not a guarantee for healing. Each person is accountable for his or her own relationship with God based on genuine trust and faith in the transforming grace, power, and work of God through His Son, Jesus Christ.

We believe that with the person of Christ, along with proper understanding of God's word, a struggling believer can be transformed from a wounded, carnally-natured Christian into a Christ-like, new-natured Christian.

The carnal nature with its associated wounds and defilements to the personal spirit often carry psychological and emotional symptoms. Terms used in explaining these principles may have been used or are used in secular counseling, therapy, or training. The use of such terms in explaining these Biblical principles do not indicate or infer that these teachings are a mental health program sanctioned or licensed by any state or national mental health licensing board.

If you are uncomfortable with this Biblical approach in healing spiritual, psychological, emotional wounds, and behavioral issues and you believe you need to be evaluated by a mental health professional, we recommend that you contact your family physician or a mental health referral agency as soon as possible.